HELPING
YOUR
DIFFICULT
CHILD
BEHAVE

HELPING YOUR DIFFICULT CHILD BEHAVE

A Guide to Improving Children's Self-Control—Without Losing Your Own

MICHAEL SCHWARZCHILD, Ph. D.

PRIMA PUBLISHING

Prima Publishing™ is a trademark of Prima Communications, Inc.

Typography by Archetype Book Composition
Interior design by Linda Shapiro
Cover design by Lindy Dunlavey, The Dunlavey Studio, Sacramento

Copy editor: Kathryn Hashimoto
Project editor: Leslie Yarborough

Library of Congress Cataloging-in-Publication Data

Schwarzchild, Michael.
    Helping your difficult child behave: a guide to improving children's self-
    control—without losing your own
Michael Schwarzchild.
        p. cm.
    Includes index.
    ISBN 1-55958-704-0
    1. Problem children.   2. Discipline of children.   I. Title.
HQ773.S52 1995
649´.64—dc20   94-39011
                                                              CIP

95 96 97 98 99 RRD 10 9 8 7 6 5 4 3 2 1
Printed in the United States of America

How To Order
Single copies may be ordered from Prima Publishing, P.O. Box 1260BK, Rocklin, CA 95677; telephone (916) 632-4400. Quantity discounts are also available. On your letterhead, include information concerning the intended use of the books and the number of books you wish to purchase.

To my wife, Karen Schwarzchild, who took me to New Orleans to write; to Jennifer Schwarzchild, Justin Virga, Jason Virga, and my other family members, all of whom feel perfectly comfortable ignoring my professional advice; to the memory of my grandmother, Belle Schwarzchild, who was always most supportive; and to all the families who have contributed to the ongoing development of this approach to helping children behave.

Contents

CHAPTER **8**
Single Parents, Divorce, Ex-Partners, and Stepfamilies

CHAPTER **9**
School-Based Programs

CHAPTER **10**
Three Case Studies

CHAPTER **11**
Troubleshooting

Preface
or
Who Do I Think I Am to Tell You How to Raise Your Kids?

Another book on improving children's behavior? Aren't there already more than enough of them on the shelves? What could possibly convince you to choose mine? My experience with children's problems didn't even start until I had been a clinical psychologist for several years. I had been interested in working with individual adults, but doing psychotherapy with these grown-ups led me into doing psychotherapy with couples. Couples, I found, often came fully equipped with children. Parents occasionally (every session) mentioned that their kids' behavior was not exactly perfect. I tried to help. . . and I was hooked for life.

There was a lot for me to think about when I added kids to my practice. In psychotherapy with adults, I try to let my clients guide the direction of our work. Many children, however, are unable or unwilling to accept such a grown-up responsibility. This situation is especially difficult with children whose behavior is genuinely dangerous.

A good example is the boy who is brought to therapy because he sticks his fingers into the spinning blades of an electric fan. With time, energy, and luck, I might discover what causes this behavior and help the child to understand and stop it. That often lengthy process, however, could have a high cost in lost and damaged fingers! It became apparent that there were times when my first goal would be to eliminate the negative behaviors. The underlying causes could then be examined under less frantic and less dangerous circumstances. This strategy has proven its value in cases where children's behavior, whether dangerous or not, has led to physical, emotional, or social problems.

I began to explore the methods my colleagues were using to change children's behavior. These were usually based on the work of well-known learning theorists, such as B. F. Skinner and Albert Bandura. In 1983, I started to use the traditional tools, such as star charts, time-outs, and various combinations of rewards and punishments. The families with whom I was working would try a recommended approach for a week and then report back to me about their results. At first, things went very well. _Everything_ worked, and I looked like a genius. This kids' stuff was kids' stuff!

For exactly one week. Parents would come back the following week to report that success had turned into failure. _Nothing_ worked, just like in the allowance systems that the parents had put together without my "invaluable" help. So much for genius! Now what? My choices were: 1) to insist that the old approaches, designed by experts, _had_ to work (making myself look pretty foolish), 2) to give up and say that I didn't have a clue (making myself look really foolish), or 3) to try to find new methods that would be more effective (at the risk of making myself look unbelievably foolish in the attempt). I decided that it was worth risking what little pride I had left to lose.

The families were remarkably willing to experiment with new techniques. If they tried an approach and it didn't improve their children's behavior, then we would scrap it and brainstorm until we came up with something else to try. Our agreement was to keep what worked and to discard what didn't, even if our results contradicted the experts' opinions. This book is the result of that still-continuing experiment.

The process of developing this approach to helping children behave never comes to an end. Every family is truly unique. Whenever I set out to design a behavioral program with a family, I encounter problems that never came up before and that require creative solutions. This ongoing evolution makes it impossible to present a "final" version of the program.

The approach described here has become the standard framework for my behavioral work with families. If you follow these directions, the program will customize itself to the particular needs of your family. I suggest that you read through the book completely before you start your own design. Then try the approach without making any changes. You may find that it meets your needs as it is presented, or you may want to tinker with it later. Just take what you need and leave the rest.

Who do I think I am to tell you how to raise your kids? A few years ago, a fourteen-year-old girl was brought to my office by her parents. The family conflict had reached a new peak several days earlier when she had thrown an open bottle of nail polish remover out her second-floor window. Big deal? Well, yes, if you consider that she had scored a direct hit on her father's brand new BMW. This was not a happy family! The story had a happy ending, though, when we used this program to help resolve the friction between parents and daughter. (Luxury car owners everywhere breathed a sigh of relief!) I've used this approach to help improve the behavior of children in dozens of families. I hope that it will help in your family as well.

Acknowledgments

With thanks to the people who helped me get ready to write this book:

> Saul Grossman, Ph.D.; Margaret Hornick, Ph.D.;
> Sam Newcomer, B.D.; Marvin Reznikoff, Ph.D.;
> and Estelle Weinrib, M.S.W.

With thanks to the people who helped me in writing this book:

> Mark Mentovai, Susan Mentovai,
> Karen Schwarzchild, and Richard Schwarzchild.

With thanks to the people at Prima Publishing who helped me get this book into your hands:

> Alice Anderson, Karen Blanco,
> Kathryn Hashimoto, and Leslie Yarborough.

And with thanks, again, to the all the families who have taught me so much about "helping your difficult child behave."

CHAPTER 1

Introduction

"We just don't know what to do, Doc. We've tried *everything,* and absolutely *nothing* works. We've tried:

1. talking,
2. reasoning,
3. star charts,
4. time-outs,
5. scolding,
6. yelling,
7. threatening,
8. sending them to their rooms,
9. taking away their privileges,
10. grounding,
11. spanking,
12. hitting,
13. sending them to camp and then moving without leaving a forwarding address

—but the kids don't even seem to care. We're at the end of our rope. What can we do?"

It's likely that at least some of this sounds familiar to you. Trying to help children behave can be very frustrating when nothing you do seems to work. But you haven't given up quite yet, or you wouldn't be reading this book and getting ready to try one more time. Don't give up! If what you've been doing hasn't been working, it's time to stop doing it and try something else.

The systematic approach to improving children's behavior that is presented here has been developed over many years of working with families. It will help to reduce conflict between you and your children, decrease the number of disagreements that you and your partner have over discipline, and eliminate the use of physical punishment in your home.

As you read through this book, you may find that some of the material is familiar. The approach described here has its roots in well-established principles of learning. Tools such as star charts (grids on which a child's behavioral successes are displayed with stars or other markers) and time-outs (periods during which a child is kept away from sources of positive reinforcement) have often been recommended to parents who are having difficulties with their children. You may even have tried some of these techniques in the past with little or no success. It is important to note that, through the process of trial and error, most of the traditional tools mentioned in this book have been changed. They are used here in ways which will be new to you.

Although the aim of this system is to shape children's behavior, it has equally important effects on the behavior of parents. The basic idea is for you to develop a truly consistent, unified approach to discipline. When the program is complete, parents become equal and interchangeable in dealing with their children's behavior. This requires a great deal of ongoing communication between parents in designing, running, and fine-tuning the program. Parents must talk about the system daily in order to deal with unforeseen situations, to share information about how the children are responding, and to prevent themselves from undermining each other. There is no avoiding the fact that improving children's behavior requires work. Keep in mind, however, that you have already been doing *plenty* of work with little progress to show for it. The approach described here will help you redirect your energy toward gaining positive results.

This program has been especially helpful in work with children who have attention-deficit hyperactivity disorder (ADHD), Tourette's disorder, oppositional and defiant behaviors, and negative school behaviors. It has demonstrated its value in the treatment of ADHD and Tourette's disorder whether or not medication has also been prescribed. The program's consistent structure helps children with these disorders to increase the control they have over their behavior, as discussed in Chapter 3.

Your child doesn't need to have a problem with a professional name in order to benefit from this approach, however. Chapter 7 shows that it is just as useful for constructing simple, sensible allowance systems that will actually get the kids to do their chores and homework without the usual procrastinating, whining, stamping, screaming, and door slamming. (Does it sound like there might be some similarities between your household and mine?)

While many problems may be solved through the use of this book, not all are suitable for such an approach. This method is designed to improve *behavior,* not to directly change thoughts or feelings. For example, it should not be used as the only treatment for a child whose main problem is depression or anxiety. These conditions require consultation with a psychologist, psychiatrist, social worker, or other helping professional who works with children and their families. Chapter 11 furnishes information about how to find a therapist or counselor. The program may be used to improve children's behavior during such treatment if the practitioner agrees that it is appropriate.

That having been said, I *have* found that improvements in kids' behavior are almost always accompanied by improvements in their general attitude (see Chapter 3). This system provides children with a variety of experiences that build self-esteem. Successes, rewards, praise, and a sense of mastery over behavior will all contribute to a child's positive attitude and self-image.

I have occasionally been asked whether this program can be used to combat children's fascination with the clothing, hairstyles, friends, music, reading material, videos, or television shows that their parents find objectionable. I am sure that this can be done. After all, jungle cats can be taught to jump through hoops of fire, something that I believe they seldom do when left to their own devices! In my opinion, however, this type of coercion would not be an appropriate use of the program. It is designed to influence negative behavior, not to decide questions of taste. I suspect that the first argument about style took place between Adam and Eve on one side, and Cain and Able on the other. (My guess would be something about hair length.) You are left to carry on this noble tradition of trying to resolve the unresolvable through example, reasoned discussion, begging, and loud sighing. Hey, eventually they'll grow out of it!

This approach is appropriate for children of all ages who are living with one or more parents or guardians. The form of the program is the same regardless of the child's age. Target Goals, Rewards, and Penalties are tailored to the specific needs of each child and family, allowing the method to be used with children from preschool through adolescence.

Couples in which each parent has a different style of discipline will find this program especially useful. Children often say that one parent is "hard" and the other is "soft," though they won't usually disclose the ways in which they can manipulate this situation to their advantage. Most parents in these families are aware of how the children try to play them against each other. ("Dad, can I keep a boa constrictor in my room? No? But *Mom* said I could." Sound familiar?) I have found that if either the hard style or the soft style is applied consistently, behavior improvement will usually follow. I have also found that the *most* successful approach is for parents to negotiate a compromise between their different styles. This creates a consistent and unified parenting style in which each partner's original position finds some degree of expression. The method described here is designed to make parents identical in matters of discipline. It also eliminates the impossible task of each parent coming up with sensible and consistent punishments at times when tempers are flaring.

Why do children exploit the differences between their parents? As maddening as it can be, I believe that this behavior reflects a critically important task in the development of mentally healthy adults. The skills that children learn through manipulating their parents are the same ones that will allow them to successfully satisfy their grown-up needs. It is a child's job to reach for as much freedom and control as possible, even through exploiting loopholes in parental discipline. It is the parents' job to allow children to get what they need without letting them get everything they want. The limits that parents provide will teach children about the real boundaries they will encounter in the adult world. In this way, children learn socially acceptable ways of satisfying their needs.

Why would children respond positively to the limits that their parents place upon them? The natural assumption is that they would react to the idea of going along with such parental boundaries by kicking and screaming every inch of the way. Despite the fact that this may often be the case, it has been my experience that children will ultimately accept such guidance. I have been amazed to find that almost all children actually welcome the change to consistent parenting that is brought about through clearly defined limits. They are certainly going to do their best to prevent you from discovering this truth, however. When freedom is offered, children (as well as grown-ups and pets) will make a grab for it. What kids would ever admit that they want and need restrictions from their parents? Nonetheless, many children have waited years for their parents to develop clear rules and consequences for behavior in the household. There is too much confusion for kids when they can never be sure of how their parents will respond to a given situation. I have come to believe that, "deep-down," children know that parents are supposed to make the rules, and kids are supposed to follow them. Any variation in this formula will lead to behavioral problems for the children and conflict for the adults.

It is worth noting that children sometimes display negative behavior in an attempt to *cause* their parents to set some limits, even though they will usually complain when these boundaries are enforced. The idea here is that kids who take on such a role may really be acting as family therapists. Their conscious or unconscious reasoning is that, if the misbehavior becomes severe enough, their parents will surely have to work together in taking control of the family. By the same token, children can misbehave in an attempt to draw attention away from their parents' conflicted relationship. These kids make this sacrifice in order to prevent their parents from becoming further estranged. Parents may unconsciously support this strategy since, if a difficult child's behavior improves, long-ignored problems in the couple's relationship might become the focus of attention. Grown-ups should make sure that their children never have to act as therapists for the family.

This book is not just for couples who are raising their own children. As discussed in Chapter 8, single parents, divorced parents, and stepparents will find the approach just as useful. Stepparents can use the program to develop a consistent and unified parenting style, a task which is often difficult in newly blended families. This method is also a powerful tool for improving behavior in the classroom, the subject of Chapter 9. When a child is exposed to similar programs at home and in school, consistency in discipline is increased and progress is speeded. Teachers and other helping professionals who are familiar with this approach can recommend it to parents who might need some help at home. Therapists and counselors can use it as a proven framework for designing behavioral programs with families.

Finally, not every approach works with every child or family. If you encounter major difficulties in constructing and running this program, or if you are not satisfied with your results, please review Chapter 11 and consider discussing the situation with someone who specializes in working with children and their families.

CHAPTER 2

*T*arget Goals, Rewards, and Penalties

What is your child doing wrong that needs to be stopped? What is your child not doing that should be started? What chores are the kids doing, and should they be doing more? The answers to these three simple questions, and the two more which follow, will form the basis for this entire approach to improving children's behavior. Though the questions might be simple, they will require some real work to answer.

THE THREE LISTS

Your first job will be to construct a list of the behaviors that you want to change. This list, called "Target Goals," consists of all the things that your child should stop or start doing, and the household chores that ought to be your child's responsibility. These chores include any jobs that the child is already doing, as well as other, age-appropriate duties that the child would take care of, without even being asked, if we were all in heaven. You should make sure that you list some easy chores as well. These will guarantee that your child experiences an immediate feeling of success as soon as the program starts.

In constructing this list, the rule is that anything goes. This is your wish list. Include as many different items as come to mind, and use your own language. Don't rule out items that might appear to be too picky, silly, hopeful, or wild. We will narrow down and focus this list more sharply in a later step. Even if some of your items are not used in the final version, they can provide information that might be helpful in the design process. Examples of Target Goals, and of items from the two other lists that you will be constructing, will be presented later in this chapter. Information about constructing lists for school-based systems is provided in Chapter 9, "School-Based Programs".

If you are part of a couple that is living together, then *you must sit down TOGETHER and construct this list, and the two that follow, TOGETHER!* Trial and error has made it very clear that when only one parent in a couple constructs the lists and the other parent just checks, edits, or accepts them, absolute failure is absolutely guaranteed. *Do it TOGETHER!* (Do you sense that I feel strongly about this?)

Months after writing the last paragraph, an event took place in my office that caused me to review my strong emphasis on couples working together. I ended up back at the same place where I had started, but I learned a few things on the way. I had sent a couple home to make their three lists with my usual insistence that they do it together. The following week, they came in with lists that were constructed entirely by mom and approved entirely by dad. I told them that our work together was now finished. They objected strongly to this news until I explained that, by continuing in this manner, they would waste hundreds of their dollars on a project that was doomed to failure. When they asked why I was so sure that the program couldn't be successfully designed their way, I answered that years of trial and error experience had been my teacher. I said that I was sure I could come up with a theory to explain why it worked this way, but that it wouldn't change the fact that failure would be the end result.

As soon as they left, I found myself wondering just what such a theory might be. It occurred to me that parents who couldn't invest even a little time together at the beginning of this project would never be able to support each other in the hard work to come. This first homework assignment is an excellent barometer of a couple's commitment to meaningful change in the family system. Good stuff.

Items about which parents disagree (a rare occurrence) should still be included on the list at this stage. Single parents should make the list by themselves, as should divorced parents who will be running the program in only one household (see Chapter 8, "Single Parents, Divorce, Ex-Partners, and Stepfamilies"). If divorced parents will be using the program in both households, and if the level of conflict between them is sufficiently low, they should construct the list together. This can lead to a degree of cooperation that may have been unheard of during the course of the marriage!

When working with parents in my office, I stress the importance of their spending a good deal of time in developing this list and the two that follow. I suggest that the experience can often be made more pleasant by the addition of candlelight and vintage wine (not too much, now). Time invested at this stage of the construction will pay off in great savings of time and energy later on.

The second list is called "Rewards." It should include everything that your child would consider to be a prize. The easiest way to come up with items for this list is to think of things or activities that the child would be willing to work for, such as toys, money, or trips to the library (yes, this actually *is* rewarding to many children). Even Rewards that might not seem appropriate should be included at this stage. Candy, for example, is something that I almost never use as a Reward, but it appears on many lists made by the parents of younger children. If something turns your child on, put it in. The idea is to generate as large a list of Rewards as possible. I recommend that you consult freely with your kids about this list. It's an un-usual child who won't tell you exactly what Rewards he or she wants.

I mentioned in the Preface that the evolution of this program makes it impossible to present a "final" version. Something new is always going on. Long after I wrote the previous paragraph, the parents of a nine-year-old boy in-cluded an item on their Rewards list that brought our session to a screeching halt. Their son's first choice of money wasn't at all unusual, but I really wasn't prepared for his request that *earrings* come next. He had a pierced ear, you see, and mom just wouldn't allow him to borrow her diamond stud. I can adapt to this, but I think I've gotten old.

The final list is called "Penalties." Just as you might ex-pect, it consists of items that your children will experience as punishment for negative behavior. Many of these conse-quences will be the opposites of those on the Rewards list. Others should be added as well, but be forewarned that this is usually the hardest of the lists to construct. Your child should *not* be consulted about this list—kids tend to choose rather lenient Penalties for themselves. As before, anything that you can think of should be included at this stage. Any-thing *but* physical punishment, that is. This approach to changing children's behavior *never* makes use of spanking, hitting, shaking, grabbing, pinching, arm twisting, or any other physical punishment. In fact, as discussed in Chapter 4, "The Consequences," this approach is designed to make such ac-tions unnecessary.

Bryan

Now for the promised examples. In order to demonstrate how the Target Goals, Rewards, and Penalties lists are con-structed, I have invented a hypothetical child. It has been my experience that hypothetical children are by far the easiest to raise. They require no food or clothing, and they always respond *perfectly* to behavioral improvement programs. The hypothetical child that I will present is actually a composite, based on the many real children with whom I have worked. The lists are made up of genuine items that were brought in by their real, non-hypothetical parents.

We will follow our child through the entire design and implementation of this program. Reference will be made to other children of differing ages and with a variety of behavioral problems when further examples might be helpful. Please keep in mind that, although the child we will be discussing has a formal, psychiatric diagnosis, your child doesn't need one in order for you to make use of this method. The same approach is used to address behavioral problems of greater or lesser severity than those presented in the following examples.

We will name our new child "Bryan." He is an eight-year-old boy who has always been highly distractible and physically active in school. His parents tell me that he has both good days and bad days at home. During the latter, he becomes extremely oppositional, defiant, and insulting. He often refuses to do such things as take a bath or go to bed. Worst of all, Bryan is prone to severe temper tantrums when he feels frustrated by his parents' requests to start or stop doing things. These tantrums occasionally escalate to the point where he punches and kicks the walls or door when sent to his room, several times leaving holes. Bryan frequently cries and screams at bath time, and he almost always stalls as much as possible at bedtime. He recently visited a neurologist, who has diagnosed him as having an attention-deficit hyperactivity disorder (ADHD). The neurologist prescribed two different medications, neither of which has had any visible effect on Bryan's behavior. Bryan is not taking medication when I begin to work with the family.

Bryan's parents, David and Kathy, argue constantly about discipline. In fact, they have been doing this since

Bryan was three years old. David is characterized as being the "hard" disciplinarian, and Kathy as the one who gives up more easily. Mom is said to frequently "undo" punishments, such as restriction of privileges or "grounding" to the house, before they are scheduled to end. Bryan admits that he can make this happen by constantly whining to her.

David feels that Kathy isn't consistent in her approach to Bryan, who therefore doesn't recognize that the consequences for negative behavior are to be taken seriously. Much of the parents' conflict takes place at night, when David returns home from work and criticizes Kathy's parenting skills. She finds this to be especially endearing after a full day of dealing with one temper tantrum after another. In a couple's session, David surprises Kathy by admitting that he can take Bryan's problems less seriously than she, because he escapes each day to the "safety" of his office. She is a lone warrior every morning and afternoon.

The couple describes the usual steps that they take when Bryan misbehaves. First comes a verbal warning. If there is no response, this is followed by a ten-minute time-out in Bryan's room. Next, television privileges are taken away. Finally, Bryan is required to come home directly from school and is grounded. David says that he has recently abandoned these steps in favor of immediately taking away all of Bryan's privileges when there is any trouble. He feels justified in doing this since Kathy frequently criticizes him for his lack of patience with Bryan anyway.

There has been some discussion between the parents about the possibility of putting a lock on Bryan's door to keep him in his room during time-outs and punishments. Kathy admits to hitting Bryan with a belt on two occasions, causing herself tremendous guilt about how she had hurt and scared him. David acknowledges that he spanked Bryan several times. Both parents are convinced that physical punishment has no long-term effect on Bryan's behavior whatsoever.

After hearing the details of the family's situation, I start considering whether to design a behavioral improvement program with them. Aside from his mild hyperactivity and attentional difficulties, Bryan doesn't appear to have any other major psychological problems, such as depression or anxiety. Since it is his *behavior* that is getting him into trouble, we decide that it would be appropriate and worthwhile to develop a program. Bryan's parents agree to stop all physical punishment in favor of trying this new approach.

Although I usually begin by having the parents prepare the Target Goals, Rewards, and Penalties lists, in this case I first ask Bryan to tell me what Rewards he would be willing to work for. Money is at the top of the list, as it frequently is. (Much more will be said in Chapter 4 about the use of money as a Reward.) It is followed by Lego blocks and building sets, video games, posters, key chains (yes, he said key chains), and troll dolls.

We then discuss his current allowance setup. He is supposed to get two dollars a week for doing a minimum number of chores. This happens only on the few occasions when 1) he does the chores and 2) his parents remember to give him his allowance (sound familiar?). Bryan wants a raise. I tell him that it might be possible for him to get more money, but he would have to take on some additional responsibilities in return. He thinks this would be fine, especially if there were a way to stop his parents from spanking him. I tell him that this has already been discussed with his folks and that he should consider it a "done deal." Bryan is thrilled with the turn of events. His program hasn't even started and he has already gotten a reward! He becomes quite anxious to begin "for real."

At this point, most of our sessions begin to involve the couple rather than Bryan. I bring him in occasionally for an individual session, or I "touch base" with him before or after some of his parents' sessions. These times are used to let him know how the program is developing and to increase his enthusiasm for it. Our focus is usually on how easy it will be for him to "make out like a bandit."

I then assign the three lists to Bryan's parents as homework. After explaining what is needed for each list, I ask that they have them ready for our next, weekly session. I beg them not to leave the construction until the last minute, since the quality of the entire program will be based on this one week's work. There is some emphasis placed on the idea that good work now will mean much less work later. Nothing like applying a little pressure! The following week, David and Kathy present me with their three lists. The first one looks like this:

Target Goals

1. Bryan will have a better attitude. He's always so negative, and sometimes he's just nasty. (This could be the universal item, since it appears on more lists than not. Judging by that fact, there seems to be some evidence that American children may have a widespread attitude problem.)

2. Bryan needs to listen to us. Sometimes, talking to him is like talking to the wall. (By the same token, American children also appear to have a widespread hearing problem.)

3. He's got to get ready for bed on time and stay in bed once he's there. He stalls and then gets out of bed over and over again. Sometimes he's up until after midnight. (A popular item.)

4. Bryan must stop lying to us. (Another popular item.)

5. We can't get him to do his homework without a major struggle. And even when he does it, he often doesn't turn it in at school the next day. (Come to think of it, most of these items are quite popular.)

6. Bath time is a nightmare. He should take his bath without having a tantrum every time.

7. If you think bed and bath times are miserable, you should be around in the morning. We can't get him up, he won't wash his face or brush his teeth, and it's almost impossible to get him to the school bus by 8:10. He wants to watch television instead of getting ready for school.

8. Every once in a while, we get a report from school that Bryan is either wandering around the classroom at the wrong times, distracting other students, or fighting. Even though we know that he has ADHD, and it's sometimes tough for him to concentrate, we'd like him to have better control over his classroom behavior.

9. His room is always a mess. For that matter, any place that he has been is always a mess. Bryan never puts anything away.

10. The temper tantrums have to stop. When he has a tantrum, Bryan absolutely won't take "no" for an answer. He says horrible things. He often hits and kicks the walls and doors, and he sometimes throws things.

11. He hits his younger sister. We want him to stop hitting.

12. His chores are to take out the garbage, clear the table after dinner, feed the dogs, and put his clean laundry away.

Well, it certainly looks as though Kathy and David's plate is full. Although there is an infinite variety of Target Goals, this is a good model for the kinds of lists that parents produce. Keep in mind that your list might be larger or smaller and that it will reflect your family's particular situation.

Other popular items for children of around eight years old include being polite, bringing personal property home from school, not tattling on siblings, not whining or screaming at parents, not automatically saying no to everything, and not getting into trouble on the school bus. Lists for younger children often include not grabbing toys from others and not entering rooms without knocking. Actually, the latter problem appears on lists for children of all ages, right up to the point where they finally leave home and end the embarrassing possibilities of doors being flung open unexpectedly. (Is it possible that I might have had a problem with this in *my* household?)

Target Goals for older children frequently include items about helping with general household chores, responding when spoken to (an example of the aforementioned hearing problem), not making plans unless parents are consulted first, not mocking or otherwise imitating parents, and not using other family members' personal property without permission. Although I have attached these examples to particular age ranges, they often appear in the lists of older or younger children as well.

Next, we examine Kathy and David's second list:

Rewards

1. Money. (Perhaps the root of all evil, but by far the most frequently requested Reward for children of all ages. And their parents. And their psychologists.)
2. Legos. (Not an endorsement, just a fact.)
3. Troll dolls. (As above.)
4. Being taken out to eat.
5. Being allowed to choose a rental videocassette.
6. Going to watch his father play touch football on weekends.
7. Being read to.
8. Going shopping to buy things for himself.

Apparently, Bryan's parents aren't aware of his fascination for key chains! If the number of possible Target Goals is infinite, the number of Rewards suggested by parents and children is at least twice infinite. In Bryan's age group, frequently mentioned items include going to the movies, buying or renting video games, going to a restaurant, staying up later than usual, and buying trading cards, toys, books, or candy. Trips to the playground, arts and crafts projects, and watching television often appear on the Rewards lists of younger children. Older children like going to the mall, having friends sleep over, telephones, extended curfews, driver's licenses, and Ferraris. Did I mention that *everyone* likes money?

The third list that Bryan's parents bring in looks like this:

Penalties

1. Time alone in his room.
2. No television.
3. No video games.
4. No playtime with friends after school. (The question of whether limits on time with friends should be used as a Penalty will be discussed in Chapter 4.)

Since they have spent so many years focused almost entirely on disciplining Bryan, David, and Kathy are quite surprised that they could come up with only four entries for the Penalties list. My experience has been that this is not at all unusual. As I mentioned previously, it is almost always the most difficult of the three lists to construct. Many Penalties lists are made up of items that are the opposites of those on the Rewards list. In Bryan's case, for example, these could include the taking away of money, Legos, or troll dolls. Other frequently mentioned Penalties involve restrictions on privileges such as using the telephone, stereo, television, or car. Not being allowed to sleep over at friends' houses or to have friends sleep over is penalizing to most children. Grounding and curfews appear on many lists.

Stop!

All right, all right. I'll admit that was pretty dramatic. Sort of like those standardized tests in school. You remember: "Don't turn this page until you are told to do so. . ."

This is the part where I totally confuse you by telling you to ignore my previous instructions. I very clearly said that you should read through this entire book before starting to design your own behavioral program. Well, forget it. At this point, you need to stop reading (*terrible* advice for an author to be giving) in order to prepare the Target Goals, Rewards, and Penalties lists for your own child. The question of what to do if you have more than one child will be dealt with in Chapter 7. At this point, make your lists for only the child who is having the most difficulty.

Chapter 3, "Operational Definition," deals with narrowing down the three lists. If you read it before actually constructing your lists, you will be tempted to skip this first step of generating as many items as possible. *Don't do it!* Great confusion lies in that direction. (In 1892, Captain Jonathan Spaulding ignored this advice with the result that he lost his entire personal fortune shortly before losing his life in a tragic plumbing accident. Or was that for breaking a chain letter? Oh, well.)

First things first. Construct the three lists now, and then read on. I'll wait for you, I promise. I've got plenty of things to do here to keep me busy until you get back. And please, if you're part of a couple, design the lists together. Did I mention that before?

CHAPTER **3**

*O**perational Definition*

Welcome back. I see that you've completed the three lists, and it's obvious that you have put a great deal of time and attention into them. I certainly appreciate the fact that all of the couples using this book *did* work together on constructing the lists (and to think that I was concerned about this). As I hinted in Chapter 2, your work on the lists is not quite finished.

ATTITUDE AND BEHAVIOR

Let us turn again to Bryan and his family in order to see what remains to be done. The first entry on their Target Goals list, "Bryan will have a better attitude," provides an excellent example. David and Kathy are concerned about Bryan's bad attitude, which they obviously want to change into a good attitude. But what does this actually mean? We certainly know that they object to the insulting things he says to them. Is that what they mean by a bad attitude, or do they also include Bryan's stomping, snorting, sighing, whining, body language, and so forth? We are suffering here from a lack of precise definition in the Target Goal.

In this case, the lack of definition takes two forms. The first involves the question of changing a child's attitude. As mentioned earlier, this program is designed to improve behavior, not attitude. Unless it's an activity that the child is *doing* (or should be doing), it can't be directly modified by this approach. The easiest way to decide if something fits the definition of behavior, rather than attitude, is to determine whether it can be seen, heard, or felt. (Please forgive me for not even thinking about children's problems that involve taste or smell!) People's actions, which can be directly perceived by our senses, are behaviors. Attitude is an abstract idea that can only be inferred from behavior. Bryan's parents can hear his words (speaking is behavior), which lead them to make assumptions about his attitude. They will be able to change the way he speaks, but not necessarily the way he feels. The first Target Goal on Bryan's list needs some work.

That having been said, I now want to take part of it back *(again?)*. Although I clearly stated that attitude cannot be directly influenced by this method, I have found that it usually changes for the better as behavior improves. When children are praised and rewarded for controlling their behavior or for taking care of their responsibilities, they have an experience of success. This generates highly rewarding, positive feelings, which increase as a child's successes multiply. In this program, each achievement whets the child's appetite for another. The easy chores on the Target Goals list provide children with an immediate sense of accomplishment. These mastery experiences boost self-esteem, and I have found that higher self-esteem leads to improvements in general attitude.

Now we face the second problem in defining Bryan's initial Target Goal. Although I said that attitude can't be changed directly, we can't just ignore the fact that Kathy and David included Bryan's bad attitude on their list. While trying to figure out how to deal with this, I conclude that I really don't know exactly what they mean by "bad attitude." Everyone uses the term. I *kind of* know what they mean. But, *specifically*, how do they know that he has a bad attitude? What defines it? With my many years of psychological training and practice behind me, I turn to a highly advanced, professional, technical tool to find out the answers. Yes—I ask!

Bryan's parents initially find these questions very difficult to answer. Like me, they have a general sense of what
goes into a bad attitude ("You know, his *attitude* is bad . . .").
I continue to ask them exactly what *behaviors* they are talking
about. However we approach this question, the answer always involves the things that Bryan says. The verbal insults,
usually muttered just loudly enough to be heard ("Whatever.
Right, Ma. You know everything, Ma."), are the most distin-
guishing characteristic of his bad attitude. Although David,
Kathy, and I agree that there is more to it than this, Bryan's
mocking is the behavior that bothers them the most. They feel
that eliminating it would lead to a more peaceful and pleasant environment for everyone in the household. The first Target Goal has just been established. Bryan is to stop insulting
his parents when they say something that he doesn't like.

DEFINING THE TARGET GOALS

The process just described is technically called "operational
definition." An abstract trait, such as attitude, is defined as
narrowly as possible by the *behaviors* that make it up. These
behaviors are always events that can be perceived by the
senses. The nasty things that Bryan says can be heard by his
parents. While it is true that a bad attitude is made up of
more than just the things that a child says, for our purposes it
is important to determine the behavior that is *most* characteristic of the general problem.

This sharp focus is necessary for two reasons. First,
without such clear definition, it is impossible to know exactly
how to improve negative behavior. In Bryan's example, what
might we do to change his attitude? Ask him to change it?
Beg him to change it? Threaten him if he doesn't change it? I
know a highly effective way to stop his insults (the very program you are reading about), but I don't have any idea how
to directly repair his bad attitude. Second, if a Goal is not

stated precisely and in terms of behavior, there is no way of knowing whether or not it has been reached. I can't tell you the exact moment that a bad attitude becomes a good one, but I certainly know when insults stop. This program requires such exactness, so that there is never a question as to when children will be given Rewards or Penalties.

Many parents think that I carry operational definition to a ridiculous extreme. I agree, and I do it because I think it's absolutely necessary. The best example of why this is so is found in "The Great Garbage Pail Scenario" (TGGPS). You are all familiar with this one. One of Junior's jobs is to empty the kitchen garbage pail into the outside garbage pail. The perpetual argument concerns when this is to be done. As parents, you have clearly stated that the garbage is to be taken out when the pail is full. A simple concept, no? You have noticed, however, that said garbage is frequently found in a column extending vertically above the pail for several feet before cascading gracefully into concentric rings around the kitchen. When you ask Junior, in the calm, patient, and measured tones for which you have justly become famous, why the garbage pail hasn't been emptied, he will gaze briefly at the pail, then briefly at you, and reply, without a trace of irony, "Uh, it's not full yet." Thus, the existence of Maalox.

This also explains the existence of operational definition. When the "Take Out the Garbage Chore" (TOTGC) is included as a Target Goal, I insist that it be defined down to the last apple core. I ask parents and child to agree on *exactly* what constitutes a full pail. If necessary, I require that the "Top of the Garbage Height" (TOTGH) be set at a particular number of inches above or below the top of the pail, with or without pushing down the pile. I then decree that a ruler be hung in a convenient spot to allow all involved parties to check the TOTGH whenever necessary. Parents are absolutely the final judges of the TOTGH and always have the last word.

This extreme level of pickiness results in several bene-fits. If everyone has agreed on the TOTGH, there can be no argument when parents say that the pile has exceeded this prearranged limit. Those horrible, but brilliant, legalistic de-fenses that children offer when they sense a loophole ("But you're not counting the way the orange peels unwound un-derneath, pushing the pile up over the top. . . .") are thus avoided. The child, on the other hand, is easily able to gauge how long the pile can safely be ignored, and to prove it tri-umphantly if necessary. I must point out here that there is *always* a "Take Out the Garbage Immediately Exception" (TOTGIE) when fish or any other nasty decomposer has been served for dinner.

Each of your Target Goals must be operationally de-fined. The Goal of having your child clear the dinner table, for example, is stated too broadly. Whose dishes should be cleared? Does clearing mean bringing them to the sink, or putting them in the dishwasher? Must the table or counters be wiped by the clearer? Your responsibility is to specify *ex-actly* what you want your child to do.

In its operational definition, Target Goal #1 is narrowed from "Bryan will have a better attitude" to "Bryan will not insult his parents when they have told him to start or stop doing something." Even the insult can be operationally defined if necessary: "Saying such things as 'Whatever. Right, Ma. You know everything, Ma,' in a nasty tone will be considered an insult." You can also specify what you mean by "nasty" if leav-ing this open might lead to a later misunderstanding. As al-ways, parents are the final judges of whether the rules have been violated. In Chapter 6, "The Chart," we will discuss what should be done if a parent makes an error in judgment (yes, this *has* been known to happen).

Parents sometimes ask me whether they should include their children in the process of choosing and operationally defining the Target Goals. I believe that the initial choices should be made by the grown-ups. When the Goals are later explained to the kids, some allowance can certainly be made for limited negotiations. What is to be avoided at all costs, however, is an endless attempt to reason and compromise until everyone is completely happy.

The fact is that not everything here is designed to make your children happy. You will be making the final decisions, and you can make them when you feel that the time is right. It is _always_ helpful to listen to what your children are saying, especially if you haven't heard it before. The validation that children receive when parents pay attention to their opinions can be tremendously therapeutic by itself.

This doesn't mean that you have to give the kids everything they want, of course. Even whether or not to explain the reasoning behind the Goals is a parental prerogative. When negotiations are in good faith, and when neither side is trying to gain an unfair advantage, then at least some measure of mutual respect and teamwork can be established. Parents shouldn't fear that they will lose their disciplinary authority through this process, since they are always the ones who determine what is to be included in the final program. The adults remain in control, even when they are willing to participate in negotiations about the Target Goals, Rewards, Penalties, or any other aspect of this approach.

LISTENING

Let's get to work on operationally defining the second item that Bryan's parents include on his Target Goals list, "Bryan needs to listen to us". The walls of my office echo with this complaint. Once again, however, we are faced with the problem of not knowing exactly what David and Kathy mean by it. Does Bryan completely ignore them when they talk to him? Does he always react this way, or just when he is being asked to do things that he doesn't like? Does he respond at all, or does he pretend that he hasn't heard anything? In my experience, it's the latter that *really* drives parents wild. Are they actually saying that he just doesn't obey them? The next step depends on the answers to these questions. In Bryan's case, his parents are upset that he doesn't acknowledge having heard them. When they finally get his attention, he doesn't comply with their wishes anyway.

The first part of the problem is dealt with by changing Target Goal #2 to "Bryan will respond when his parents ask him something." Good enough? No way! If you see a possible disaster coming from leaving this Goal as it is, you're getting the hang of this. If not, you need only imagine this scene:

Kathy: (pleasantly) "Bryan, did you do your homework?"
Bryan: (30-second pause, then grunting almost inaudibly through the thundering sound of a video game) "Uh."
Kathy: (angrily) "Bryan, answer me!"
Bryan: (also angrily) "I did!"
Kathy: (more angrily) "Well, I didn't hear you."
Bryan: (insultingly) "Well, you must be deaf."
Kathy: (furiously) "DID YOU DO YOUR HOMEWORK?"
Bryan: (also furiously) "I SAID 'YES'!"
Kathy: (less furiously) "Well, I didn't hear you."

And so on. Another one of those possibly familiar household events.

What's needed to prevent this oft-repeated scenario is some further operational definition. I ask Bryan's parents how much time he should have before responding to a question. They agree that five seconds is enough. They also admit, and Bryan has told me previously, that they often call to him from distant rooms. In those situations, Bryan isn't sure that they have called, and they aren't sure that he has heard. So, Target Goal #2 is rewritten as "He will respond clearly and loudly, within five seconds, when his parents ask him something. This will only apply when his parents are in the same room with him, or when they have a clear view of him." Kathy and David will judge whether the response is acceptable and within the time limit. Picky, isn't it? But it certainly closes the loopholes.

The second part of this item involves Bryan's not carrying out his parents' wishes even when he has heard them. Unfortunately, a Goal saying "Bryan will do what we want, when we want" violates all of our rules about operational definition. Although it would be wonderful, it is much too broad, unmeasurable, and unenforceable. We decide to continue making individual Target Goals for each behavior that Kathy and David see as a problem.

THE NIGHTTIME PACKAGE

Time to move to the third item on Bryan's list, the ever-popular "Nightmare at Bedtime". Surprisingly, it is one of the easiest problems to take care of with this program. The usual, expected events in a nighttime or morning routine readily lend themselves to operational definition. "He's got to get ready for bed on time and stay in bed once he's there," was the original item that David and Kathy included on their list. As you can now imagine, I have a few questions to ask about this.

Exactly what is his bedtime? "8:30." What is he expected to do before bedtime? "Brush his teeth and pick a book to read." If he is picking a book and his bedtime is 8:30, by what time should he be in bed to read? "8:05." (*I* don't know. You'd have to ask *them* about the ":05.") Why does he keep getting up after he goes to bed? "He says he needs to go to the bathroom." Is that true? "No." What about bedtimes on weekends? "In bed to read at 8:35, lights out at 9:00." This will make you happy? "Oh, so happy!" You also have an item about taking a bath? "Oh, no! Give us a break, Doc! Okay, he needs to take a bath." When, exactly? "By 7:30 on school nights, 8:00 on weekends." And in the summer? "Enough, already! We'll deal with that in the summer." Fine. I'll just make a note of that.

Target Goal #3, The Nighttime Package, becomes "Bryan will take a bath by 7:30 P.M. on school nights and 8:00 on weekends. He will brush his teeth and pick a book by 8:05 on school nights and 8:35 on weekends. Bryan will be in bed with lights out, having gone to the bathroom, at 8:30 on school nights and 9:00 on weekends. He will *not* get out of bed after this unless it is an emergency." Of course, David, Kathy, and Bryan will later discuss the types of situations that qualify as emergencies.

LYING

The ease with which we operationally defined the bedtime routine is more than made up for by the difficulty of the next item, "Bryan must stop lying to us." The main problem here is that, unless your child has eyes that shoot sparks or a head that spins completely around during a lie, it is usually impossible for you to be sure that you're not hearing the truth. I have found that parents generally accept this as a fact of life, since they actually have no choice. By the rules of operational definition, we cannot eliminate behavior if we are not even sure that it is taking place. When they include this item on the list, however, most parents are talking about the times when they have *caught* their child lying. That's a different story.

The most common complaint is directed toward children who maintain their innocence in the face of overwhelming evidence against them (grown-ups frequently take this same approach during mishaps at work). Parents tell their children that lying just compounds the felony, since there will now be anger about both the original crime *and* the attempt to cover it up. Kids don't get this. Adults who have mishaps at work don't get this. Richard Nixon didn't get this. Target Goal #4 became "Bryan will not lie when he has been caught doing something wrong. His parents will be the final judges as to whether he is lying."

HOMEWORK

"We can't get him to do his homework without a major struggle. And even when he does it, he often doesn't turn it in at school the next day." The fifth item on Kathy and David's list of Target Goals raises a number of school-related issues. The "doing the homework" part of the equation is easily handled (honest!), since it takes place entirely within the home. It is easily handled *if* you are sure what assignments your children are being given, that is.

To operationally define homework, you must choose the exact time at which, or by which, it must be done on both weekdays and weekends. Parents *always* have to check to make sure that it has been done. Bryan has about 30 minutes of homework each night. Target Goal #5 becomes "Bryan will do his homework each night at 5:30. He will do his weekend homework before 6:00 P.M. on Sunday." Older children, who can be expected to have more homework, should be given deadlines by which it must be done.

What if your children are among those occasional few who might not let you know exactly what homework they are supposed to be doing? I have found that, if it's necessary, almost all schools and individual classroom teachers are willing to participate in a "Home/School Homework Log" system. Indeed, some schools already use this approach as a standard part of their academic programs. School personnel are usually pleased to work with highly involved parents who are trying to improve their children's classroom performance.

To ease the administrative strain on already overworked teachers, the burden of keeping this Log falls entirely on the child. In this arrangement, the *student* is completely responsible for writing down all the homework assignments as each teacher gives them out. A single page is used for a whole day's assignments. The child must have all teachers initial their respective assignments. A teachers' initials and the notation, "None," are required when there is no homework assigned. Teachers can also use the Homework Log to alert parents to upcoming tests and long-term assignments.

At home, the parents initial each assignment on the Log when they have seen the completed homework. This is a fairly foolproof approach, especially when everyone understands that any assignments without both a parent's and a teacher's initials are immediately considered to be incomplete. Further, students who forget (or "forget") to bring the Log home are treated as if they had not gotten it signed at all on that day. No questions asked.

The second half of this homework Target Goal involves Bryan's not handing in his completed assignments. There are two ways that this can be handled. First, the teacher can include a notation in the Home/School Homework Log as to whether the previous day's homework was turned in. Parents are then easily able to monitor their child's homework performance. This is the approach that David and Kathy choose. They rewrite Target Goal #5 to read, "Bryan will do his homework each night at 5:30. Weekend homework will be done before 6:00 P.M. on Sunday. He will turn in his completed assignments. He will show us his Homework Log every day after he has done his assignments." Alternately, complete responsibility for homework assignments can be taken by the school. We will look more closely at that approach in Chapter 9, "School-Based Programs."

THE MORNING PACKAGE

Bath time, the sixth item on the list, was taken care of in Target Goal #3, The Nighttime Package. The seventh item, The Morning Package, gives us another chance to go through the drill. I've found that the easiest way to deal with the morning routine is to specify a time by which *all* necessary chores are to be completed. The understanding is that these chores must be taken care of before the child can read, watch TV, play, or otherwise use the time before school. Bryan's morning responsibilities become Target Goal #6: "He will wash his face, brush his teeth, get dressed, eat breakfast, and be ready to leave the house by 8:10 A.M. on school days." This is a fairly compact list. You can also include such things as making the bed and picking up in the room if these activities are part of the morning routine in your household.

Recently, a family came up with a novel approach to setting the times by which The Morning Package must be completed. The parents had become frustrated with having to decide on different deadlines for weekdays, weekends, and summers. The problem was solved when they required that all morning items be completed before noon throughout the entire year. When school was in session, this meant that everything had to be done before their son left in the morning (a time which was written into the Goal); otherwise, the noon deadline would be missed while the child was in school. On weekends and in the summer, noon was the boy's actual time limit no matter what else was planned for the day. Elegant and effective. Bryan's folks agree that this is the way to go. If you choose not to take this approach, you must be sure to specify the different time limits for each possible situation. Deadlines for The Nighttime Package also need to be adjusted according to the day of the week and the season.

SCHOOL BEHAVIOR, ATTENTION-DEFICIT HYPERACTIVITY DISORDER, AND TOURETTE'S DISORDER

In the eighth item on their original list, Kathy and David tackle Bryan's wandering around, fighting, and distracting others in school. This is another situation that can be handled either by the parents or, as will be described in Chapter 9, by the school. We already established the framework for a home-based approach when we looked at Bryan's homework problems in Target Goal #5. The Homework Log used there can also carry notes from teachers who observe any of the negative behaviors mentioned by Kathy and David. Target Goal #7 becomes "Bryan will receive no notes from school about wandering around the classroom at the wrong times, distracting other students, or fighting."

This can be a most difficult Goal for children who, like Bryan, have ADHD. You should feel free to adjust it to the specific needs of your child. For example, it might be reasonable to accept one or more behavior reports each day, or in each class. Even several such reports can represent a genuine improvement in classroom behavior. Other problem school behaviors can also be listed in a Target Goal, but you must (of course) be specific.

This approach to improving behavior has been very helpful for children of all ages who have ADHD or Tourette's disorder. Children with ADHD can be highly distractible, experiencing difficulty in focusing their attention for long periods. They can also be *very* physically active, impulsive, and disorganized. Tourette's disorder is characterized by multiple motor tics, which, at some time, have been accompanied by at least one vocal tic. Children with Tourette's disorder can also be quite impulsive, distractible, and hyperactive.

Parents of children with these special problems will tell you that behavior control is often extremely difficult for the kids. There are mild cases, in which the symptoms are few and easily controlled, and there are very severe cases. The family chaos that can accompany the latter must be experienced to be truly understood. Although medication is often effective in improving behaviors related to these problems, it is seldom sufficient by itself. A structured and consistent parental approach to discipline, such as the one that we are developing here, is also required; in milder cases of ADHD and Tourette's disorder, it may be all that is needed. The specialists in your schools or community can help you to determine which interventions are right for your child. The Appendix contains information about some of the other resources available to help with these problems.

Lists of Target Goals for children with ADHD or Tourette's disorder often include items that apply specifically to hyperactive or impulsive behaviors. A child with ADHD, for example, might be asked not to get up from the meal table (at home or in a restaurant) more than once every fifteen minutes. Numbers such as these should always be adjusted to reflect your child's needs and capabilities. You can also decide whether or not the child should ask for your permission before leaving the table. An example of a Goal that could be helpful for children with Tourette's disorder would be to stop a heated and escalating argument for a fifteen-minute "cooling-off period" at a parent's request. The arguing parties would each go to separate, prearranged sites, returning to resume the discussion as soon as the fixed time period has elapsed. This process would continue until it was no longer necessary.

THE MESSES

Item nine on the Target Goals list should be familiar to everyone who has raised children on planet Earth. The messy room. The messy play area. The messy basement, family room, garage, driveway, yard, fill in this space with any place that your child has been. At times, I have felt that my entire career has been based on dealing with this problem. Fortunately, there are several ways that it can be handled. As we discussed before, picking up in the bedroom can be part of The Morning Package. If you would prefer, it can just as easily be included in The Nighttime Package. A completely separate Target Goal can be written for room, or other, cleaning.

The exact requirements of the picking up must be listed, of course. You will need to specify what is to be done, by what time, and on what days. This can be as simple as having the child put away enough toys so that you can actually see the floor. You might also want to include such tasks as making the bed, putting dirty laundry in the hamper, organizing shelves, and so forth. A more thorough, weekly cleaning can also be a part of this Goal if you list all the necessary details.

Bryan's parents decide to make bedroom cleaning a part of The Morning Package. Their rewritten Target Goal #6 becomes "He will wash his face, brush his teeth, get dressed, eat breakfast, clean up his room, and be ready to leave the house by 8:10 A.M. on school days, noon on other days. Room cleaning means making the bed, picking up all items that don't belong on the floor, and putting dirty laundry in the hamper."

"But," I hear you say about your messy daughter, "It's not just her room that's the problem. It's all the other places she goes. When she comes home, she leaves her (multiple choice, depending on the child's age) toys/books/clothes/art supplies/sports equipment/food/boyfriends all over the house!" Okay, not her boyfriends, but you get the general idea. This situation always appears to be very complicated because of the large number of things usually left in a larger number of places.

Over the years, a single Target Goal has emerged to cover this multitude of messes. It is the highly celebrated Scattered Items Goal. Bryan's Target Goal #8 becomes: "Bryan will put away items from one activity before starting another." Simple and effective for children of all ages. And their fathers. This Goal works for all misplaced items, including jackets and bookbags (both of which are traditionally located on kitchen floors shortly after the end of the school day), soda cans, games, homework, dishes, tools, and automobiles.

When kids are involved in long-term projects, they can certainly be allowed to leave any related items in place. If you are using the Scattered Items Goal, however, this kind of exception to the rule should *always* require parental permission.

TANTRUMS, ANGER, AND HITTING

The tenth item on the original Target Goals list involves Bryan's tantrums and his refusal to take "no" for an answer. Not surprisingly, Kathy and David's first task is to operationally define "tantrum" by describing the exact behaviors that they want Bryan to stop. Anyone who has visited a supermarket is aware that children's tantrums come in a great variety of sizes, types, and durations. Some involve throwing things and hitting. Others feature the child's saying "no" to everything, lying down, and refusing to move. Almost all include yelling. Bryan specializes in screaming, insulting, hitting, kicking, and throwing things when he is frustrated. Thus, Target Goal #9 becomes "No more tantrums. Bryan will not scream, insult, hit, kick, or throw things when he is angry."

This is *not* to say that Bryan shouldn't get angry. It is necessary and important for all of us to experience and express our feelings, even the negative ones. Since this Target Goal takes away Bryan's usual means of expressing anger, I ask his parents to talk with him about alternate ways of making his feelings known. This step is so critical that I also spend time on it in my individual sessions with Bryan.

You might have discussions with your children about such options as saying, "I'm angry!" and then telling you why. Kids can voluntarily go to their rooms to calm down. They can hit a pillow or a punching bag (I frequently recommend the latter), scream in the backyard (neighbors love this), or rant and rave in the basement (parents love this). You can even choose to allow a prearranged number of angry statements, or a given length of time, before the child is expected to use one of these other means of expression. It might also be helpful to prompt the child that another way of venting anger needs to be chosen immediately or a Target Goal will be missed. This approach, like all prompting, should only be used if it is decided upon in advance (as discussed further in Chapter 6, "The Chart").

"He hits his younger sister. We want him to stop hitting." The eleventh item is easy to turn into Target Goal #10, "No hitting." I always lobby for this to mean "no hitting anyone, anytime," but parents have a variety of opinions about self-defense. I will continue my lobbying, but your viewpoint and the school rules about hitting should be your guide. Just make sure, as always, that your expectations are clearly stated. For Bryan, this item includes not hitting his sister even when she hits him first. As in the previous Target Goal, Kathy, David, and I suggest an alternate response for this situation: Bryan is to tell his parents that he has been hit, and they will handle it from there. He is also told that his parents will weigh all of the available evidence in making their final judgment as to whether or not he has hit someone.

Well, well, well. We've finally made it to the twelfth, final, and easiest item on Kathy and David's list: the chores. We looked at the "Take Out the Garbage Chore" and clearing the dishes in our discussion of Target Goal #1. Operational definitions for feeding the dogs and putting away the clean laundry should now be child's play. Target Goal #11, The Chore Package, becomes: "Bryan will take out the garbage when it is even with the top of the can or upon a parent's request. Pushing the garbage down in the can is allowed *only* before his parents have noticed a violation. He will take his own dishes to the sink whenever he finishes eating. He will feed the dogs by 6:30 P.M. When clean laundry has been placed on his bed, he will put it away before bedtime."

I've found that the ideal number of operationally defined Target Goals for a final list is ten or less, with fifteen being the absolute maximum. More Goals than that will just overwhelm a child. If your list is too large, bear in mind that related items can often be grouped into a single Goal package. Bryan's Morning, Chore, and Nighttime Packages are good examples of this approach.

That's it. We got to the end of the list. We're done with operational definition. We did it! No more, right? Well, maybe a *little* more. There are still a few odds and ends to talk about. The most important one?

DOCTOR MICHAEL'S SPECIAL TARGET GOAL

That's not really its official name, but if I tell you what it is now, it will spoil all my fun. Let me start with a question. How many times should you have to ask your child to do something before he or she actually does it? All together now: *Once!* Did everyone give this answer? Of course you did. You're parents.

So let me ask you another question. How many times should your boss, spouse, or significant other have to ask *you* to do something before *you* actually do it? Once? Twice? Until hell freezes over? Not quite so unanimous in your answers this time, are you? We tend to expect a little more from our children than we expect from ourselves. In my case, when I've worked for other people, I've *always* done what I was asked to do *immediately*. If I really wanted to do it, that is. If I didn't, I'd probably get around to it. Eventually. Maybe. If I were reminded of it frequently. Which I'd resent terribly.

I believe that it's unrealistic for parents to expect their children to do everything on the first asking. Please don't get me wrong. It would be a wonderful world if this could happen, especially in my house. It's just not in the job description for children. As I mentioned in Chapter 1, they must test the limits of their parents' authority to see how much they can get away with in the "real" world. I tell parents that asking once is not enough, and I have them choose another number. So, how many times should you have to ask your child to do something before he or she actually does it? Make your choice before reading on.

At this point, a clear division usually develops between the "hard" parent and the "soft" one. The former sticks to saying that once is enough, twice if it absolutely can't be once, but it should still really be once. The latter makes a move to three, four, or five times, and won't look the former directly in the eye. I smile, say that they have to come to some agreement, and settle in to enjoy the process of negotiation. Over the years, I have been amazed to find that, when left to their own devices, 99.9 percent of all parents will eventually agree on the same number. The number is almost invariably three. Perhaps this is because three has always been such an important number in human culture. We have three bears, blind mice, Stooges, strikes and you're out, coins in a fountain, and so on. We now also have the real name for Doctor Michael's Special Target Goal:

THE THREE-TIME RULE

The Three-Time Rule is always the last item on the Target Goals list. For Bryan, it is Target Goal #12. It is by far the most powerful, single tool in this whole program. Like all very powerful tools, there are special instructions for its use, which must be followed to make it work properly.

It is unfortunate, but true, that no matter how carefully you have put together your Target Goals list, unexpected situations will come up. If the Target Goals include only those negative behaviors that are repetitive and fairly frequent, how should you deal with occasional disasters, the ones that only happen from time to time? The Three-Time Rule is designed to make these events part of the overall program so that they can be treated in the same way as the official Target Goals.

Here's how it works. Let's say that you want Junior to turn off the television, and he doesn't want to do it (a completely imaginary situation, of course). You ask him to turn it off. He ignores you. You ask him to turn it off. He ignores you. And so on. Even within the program that we are designing, this drama can continue as long as you and he are willing to repeat yourselves. Things change dramatically, however, at the moment that you say, "Junior, this is the Three-Time Rule. I'm telling you *once,* turn off the television." If your child is trying to please you, is easily intimidated, or has experienced the Penalties that follow violations of the Three-Time Rule, he will turn off the television at this point. He gets credit for following the Rule. If the television stays on, however, you will judge that a suitable amount of time has passed before saying, "This is the *second* time I'm telling you. Turn off the television." You do *not* have to repeat that you are now using the Three-Time Rule. If the television is turned off here, the child still gets credit for following the Rule.

If the television still remains on, there are two possible paths that you might take. This is a decision that must be made when you first design your program, since it then becomes permanent. The more conservative path is to say, "This is the *third* time that I've told you to turn off the television. You have now lost credit for the Three-Time Rule." The alternative is to say, "I'm telling you for the *third* time, turn off the television. If you don't do it *right now,* you will lose credit for the Three-Time Rule." Although either of these approaches works well, most parents have chosen the second.

It is important to keep in mind that the Three-Time Rule is *never* to be used for behaviors that are already included in the Target Goals. The Rewards and Penalties that we will be discussing shortly make this unnecessary. You would also *never* use the Three-Time Rule to prompt children about taking care of things that have already been listed in the Target Goals. They will either meet the Goals or not, and the consequences will vary accordingly. The Three-Time Rule stands by itself as a way to influence behaviors that are not already specified in your program.

As I mentioned earlier, the Three-Time Rule is a very powerful tool. It really works. By its very nature, it creates a potential problem for parents. You can easily be seduced by success into overusing it. If the Three-Time Rule is used for *every* problem that comes up, your child will surely start to ignore it. Much of its power lies in your applying it sparingly and in situations that are really important. We will shortly have an example of how the Three-Time Rule should be used.

BRYAN'S OPERATIONALLY DEFINED TARGET GOALS

In summary, here is Bryan's completed Target Goals list:

1. Bryan will not insult his parents when they have told him to start or stop doing something.

2. He will respond clearly and loudly, within five seconds, when his parents ask him something. This will only apply when his parents are in the same room with him, or when they have a clear view of him.

3. Bryan will take a bath by 7:30 P.M. on school nights and 8:00 on weekends. He will brush his teeth and pick a book by 8:05 on school nights and 8:35 on weekends. Bryan will be in bed with lights out, having gone to the bathroom, at 8:30 on school nights and 9:00 on weekends. He will *not* get out of bed after this unless it is an emergency.

4. Bryan will not lie when he has been caught doing something wrong. His parents will be the final judges as to whether he is lying.

5. Bryan will do his homework each night at 5:30. Weekend homework will be done before 6:00 P.M. on Sunday. He will turn in his completed assignments. He will show his parents his Homework Log every day after he has done his assignments.

6. He will wash his face, brush his teeth, get dressed, eat breakfast, clean up his room, and be ready to leave the house by 8:10 A.M. on school days, noon on other days. Room cleaning means making the bed, picking up all items that don't belong on the floor, and putting dirty laundry in the hamper.

7. Bryan will receive no notes from school about wandering around the classroom at the wrong times, distracting other students, or fighting.

8. Bryan will put away items from one activity before starting another.

9. No more tantrums. Bryan will not scream, insult, hit, kick, or throw things when he is angry.

10. No hitting.

11. Bryan will take out the garbage when it is even with the top of the can or upon a parent's request. Pushing the garbage down in the can is allowed _only_ before his parents have noticed a violation. He will take his own dishes to the sink whenever he finishes eating. He will feed the dogs by 6:30 P.M. When clean laundry has been placed on his bed, he will put it away before bedtime.

12. The Three-Time Rule.

Done. After you operationally define your own Target Goals, you will be ready to tackle the Rewards and Penalties.

CHAPTER 4

*T*he Consequences

How's *that* for an ominous chapter title? Not to worry, though. If we design our program well, the consequences for your children will be mostly positive. We will now discuss the Rewards and Penalties that will help you to bring about the desired improvements in your children's behavior.

Why must we talk about consequences for behavior that hasn't even happened yet? A good question, for which there are a number of good answers. First, you may have noticed that the result of inventing Penalties on the spur of the moment, and in the heat of battle, is almost always a complete disaster. Perhaps you will recognize these words as having come out of your mouth at one time or another: (Angry) "You didn't take out the garbage?" (Angrier) "Again?" (Way Angrier) "How many times have I told you to take out the garbage?" (The Big Finish) "Go to your room *right now*, AND DON'T COME OUT FOR THE REST OF YOUR LIFE!" Oops. Well, we've all been there.

One reason to specify consequences in advance is to avoid suddenly choosing Penalties that are overly harsh, too lenient, or completely nonsensical. Similarly, if you are always inventing new consequences on the spot, you are spending a good deal of your time reinventing the wheel. You don't need a new and different Penalty each time the garbage isn't taken out. The same old Penalty will do just fine, and you can be ready with it well in advance. This also helps to avoid the Surprised Spouse Scenario: "You sent him to his room FOR THE REST OF HIS LIFE?"

A related issue involves consistency between two parents who are handling discipline. Children have definite preferences about which parent they'd rather deal with when there's trouble. If mom and dad don't deliver equal justice, the kids are going to angle for the "softer" one to dish out the Penalties. That's the parent who will be handed the bad report card. By the same token, the parent with the looser purse strings will be given the good report card. Funny how that seems to happen!

If parents agree in advance on all the Rewards and Penalties to be used in a behavioral program, they tightly close the single, largest loophole that children are able to exploit. In the eyes of their children, two individual parents become one solidly unified parent when it comes to matters of discipline. It is no longer important whether it is mom or dad who responds. The consequences are now consistent between the partners. When this program is completed, each parent will be rewarding or penalizing exactly the same target behaviors in exactly the same ways and at exactly the same times. *That* is what makes the whole thing work.

BRYAN'S REWARDS

As you've probably guessed by now, the lists of Rewards and Penalties that you made up for your child are going to need a little work. Don't panic. This will be a piece of cake compared to the Target Goals. Let's go back to our friend, Bryan, to see what has to be done.

Bryan's parents have come up with eight Rewards that he will probably work for. His list consists of money, Legos, troll dolls, going out to eat, choosing a rental videocassette, watching his father play football on weekends, being read to, and shopping for himself. This list contains all the elements necessary to provide Bryan with excellent incentives for improving his behavior.

The idea here is to determine which single Reward on the list will be the most attractive to the child. Simple? Well, there are a few conditions (of course). First, the Reward has to be something that can easily be divided into seven equal parts. This is required because one piece of the total Reward will be given to the child on each day of the week that he or she accomplishes *all* of the Target Goals. The all-or-nothing daily approach that is used in this program will be discussed in Chapter 5, "The Program." We'll shortly be taking a look at why I made you construct such a long list of Rewards if we're now going to ignore everything on it that's not divisible by seven.

On Bryan's list, everything can be divided by seven except watching his dad play football on weekends. It would not be realistic, however, to provide a daily troll doll, video rental, restaurant trip, or shopping spree. Legos might qualify, since they can be given out a few at a time. Being read to is a special case that we will examine shortly. On Bryan's Rewards list, money is the item most easily divisible by seven.

The second consideration in choosing a Reward is that it can't be something that the child always gets, or should get anyway. If your family usually goes to a movie or restaurant on weekends, whether or not the kids have behaved well during the week, then these activities won't work as Rewards. The Reward has to be something that the child doesn't routinely get. As harsh as it might sound, a Reward is only effective when the child is usually deprived of it. We've all seen sea lions that have learned to honk horns in exchange for fish (yes, sir—*That's* entertainment!). They can only be taught to do this if they are hungry at the start. So don't use money as a Reward if your child is independently wealthy.

MONEY

"Money?" I hear you cry. "Money? How can you give the kid money for doing the things he's supposed to do anyway?

Isn't he part of the family? Doesn't he have responsibilities around here like everyone else? Isn't that bribery? I'm not going to bribe *my* kid. No way. Case closed." I may have heard this once or twice before. We'll keep the case open just long enough for me to make *my* case in favor of using money for this program. When a child is old enough to appreciate what money is and how it works, there are a number of factors that make it ideal as a Reward. Since Bryan is eight years old and mentioned money as his first choice, he is a likely candidate for an allowance-based program.

The first factor in favor of using money as the Reward is that it is already valuable to many children. They are usually willing to work for it, as their parents do. Kids know that money can be a useful tool in obtaining other things that they want. Second, allowance systems are common in many households, even though they generally don't work. Almost everyone is familiar and comfortable with them. Third, this Reward, in child-size portions, is fairly easy for parents to obtain and keep on hand. Fourth, once a total, weekly allowance amount is chosen, it is a simple matter to make slight adjustments so that it can be evenly divided by seven.

What about the bribery question? I used to worry about this one myself. After all, getting paid for the things that they're expected to do sounds so . . . so . . . hmmm. Actually, it sounds like what all of us do when we work for a living. You know, as much as I love my work, the chances of my showing up for it if I'm not going to be paid are *really* slim. Children being paid for carrying out their responsibilities is really not that different from what happens in their parents' work world.

Putting a child on an allowance-based system may also have hidden benefits. Many of us complain that our children don't understand the value of a dollar. Using money in this approach is an excellent way of building that understanding. Most importantly, it has been my experience that money is usually a very effective Reward. It would certainly be wonderful if children would behave and do all of their chores because they knew it was the right thing to do. The reason that you are reading this book, however, is because that hasn't been happening in your household. I recommend that, if it is attractive to your child, you consider an allowance as the daily Reward unless your are unalterably opposed to it in principle.

If you elect to use money as the Reward, you must make sure that there are no other sources of income that would make an allowance unimportant to your child. That steady drizzle of pocket money from grandpa or an ex-spouse, for example, should be cut off. Money that arrives for birthdays and major holidays is an exception if it can be kept within reason. Remember, that sea lion needs to be hungry!

In cases where your child is too young to be interested in money, or where you have decided against using it, you will need to be creative in choosing a different Reward. It must still be something that can be delivered every day. You might consider some type of token to represent a day's success. This token can have real value to younger children. Stickers, for example, work very well with the preschool and early primary school crowd. Interestingly enough, coins work very well as tokens for children who are not yet old enough to understand the actual value of money. They are still aware of the importance of cash in our culture. The bigger the coin, the better.

Legos and play money have also been successfully used as tokens. Tokens or coupons that can be exchanged for something desirable are effective with children of any age. The value of these tokens, and the goods and services that can be bought with them, should be established ahead of time. Play money or poker chips can easily be used in this way. Kids should be able to buy prizes whenever they have enough tokens.

In the unlikely event that you have a child who is old enough to appreciate the value of money but who doesn't really care about it one way or the other, just wait a bit. It's been my experience that the discovery and valuation of the opposite sex is often accompanied by some major changes in the appreciation of money. It's importance increases substantially when kids realize that they can use it to go to better places in better vehicles and in better clothes. As a side issue, I've also noticed that this romantic awakening can often bring about improvements in behavior that are beyond the skill of *any* parents or therapists. Never underestimate the value of wanting to impress someone important.

The last consideration in choosing the daily Reward is that it must be something that can be put in the child's hand, something that can be touched. This is true for children of any age, but it is especially important for younger children. Grown-ups can easily wait one or two weeks to be paid for their work. We are comfortable about putting off our gratification, and we understand that we will still be paid after such a delay. As will be discussed in Chapter 7, "A Simple Allowance System, with Siblings," Jean Piaget found that the ability to engage in abstract thinking develops as we age. Most kids do not think in this way. They live in the present, not the future, and their good behavior needs to be rewarded soon after it takes place. Putting a portion of the Reward directly in a child's hand every day provides an immediate and powerful positive message that doesn't require any abstract thinking. Making the child wait a whole week for payment is a major reason why traditional allowance systems fail so reliably.

You are responsible for having the chosen Reward on hand every day. No IOUs, no ifs, ands, or buts. If the Reward is not available when the child expects it, THIS PROGRAM WILL FAIL. A Reward is most effective when it is delivered as soon as possible after the conditions required for getting it are satisfied. Many allowance systems fail because parents frequently tell their children that they will "owe them" the money. It turns out that "the check is in the mail" doesn't fool kids, either. It's relatively easy to keep the daily amounts of any chosen Reward on hand, and it will be worth it for you to do so.

After all of that, I probably don't need to tell you that Bryan's parents decide to use an allowance as his Reward. The next question they ask is the same one that *all* parents ask at this point. "How much is right? We don't want it to be too much, but we want it to be enough." There are a number of ways of approaching this question. You should always start by asking your child how much he or she thinks is fair. Unfortunately, the answer might include several zeroes to the left of the decimal point. Try asking how much the child's friends are getting. You'll be surprised to find out that other people's children receive hundreds of dollars each month for doing practically nothing. Talking to other parents and teachers is often helpful in determining the appropriate amount for an allowance. Ultimately, the decision will be based on how much you are asking the child to do, how much you can afford, and how much the other kids are getting in your community.

In truth, there is often a surprising difference between the amount of allowance that children want and the amount that their parents think they should get. I always ask for the child's opinion separately from that of the parents. The surprise is how frequently parents are willing to give more than the child wants. This is a wonderful situation for a happy compromise, since the child can get more than he or she wanted, while the parents pay less than they expected. Children can be told that they got an "instant raise" because they will have more responsibilities. Any raise is a morale booster, and one right at the start of the program seems especially effective in developing enthusiasm.

You might also give a small raise when your division of the weekly allowance by seven doesn't come out exactly right. I always recommend that the allowance be rounded up to the nearest sensible amount of change. This is exactly what happens with Bryan. His parents decide that $5.00 is the right weekly amount for an eight-year-old boy. Having 71.429¢ on hand each night, however, would be some trick. I suggest, and David and Kathy agree, that the allowance be increased to $5.25, or 75¢ per day. Instant raise. Happy kid. Bryan's previous allowance has been $2.00 a week. Very happy kid, even though he was going to be asked to do more for his money.

THE BONUS REWARD

So, why *did* I make you come up with all those other Rewards on your list? There *must* be a good reason, right? Right. The Reward that we have been discussing is one of several that we must consider; it is the one that can be given every day. I believe that a second, *Bonus* Reward should be given at the end of a completely perfect week. A completely perfect week? That's a week in which your child successfully carries out *every* single Target Goal. Every one. Every day. For a whole week. What? Am I *crazy? A perfect week?* "We can't get this kid to do *anything,* and he's talking about a *perfect week?* We might as well have taken the money we spent on this book and thrown it at passing cars instead!"

Whew! How quickly they turn on you! At this point, you'll just have to take my word for the fact that perfect weeks are within your child's grasp. We will go ahead and choose a Bonus Reward just in case this miracle occurs. The Bonus Reward should be bigger than the daily Reward, but not so big as to stress your pocketbook. Again, it should be something that the child doesn't automatically get already, and something that will be all right for the child *not* to have if the week isn't perfect. Refer to your Rewards list and see what might be appropriate.

For Bryan, there are many possibilities. His parents think that a small troll doll or Lego toy, videocassette rental, video game rental, or cash bonus would work well. They are concerned that the same Bonus Reward week after week might become boring to him, however. How's *that* for optimism? They decided to allow Bryan to choose any one of the Bonus Rewards on their list after a perfect week. The cash Bonus Reward is set at $2.50, the approximate value of the other bonuses.

You should feel free to specify a single Bonus Reward for perfect weeks, or to use a menu like the one that Kathy and David chose. Either approach works well if the Rewards are attractive to the child. The item or items to be used, however, *must* be specified in advance. "We'll decide when we get there" is an approach that almost guarantees failure. If you are going to allow your child to select a Bonus from several alternatives, the menu of choices must be decided upon before the program starts. Depending on the age of the child, parents have used such things as extended curfews; baseball cards; books or comic books; toys; choices of video game or videocassette rentals; trips to movies, parks, playgrounds, or special restaurants; and (of course) cash as Bonus Rewards.

Don't confuse the Bonus Reward with the prizes that your kids will purchase if you are using tokens or coupons for the daily Rewards. The Bonus Reward is given *only* after a perfect week, and it would be given even if the child has also bought something else with tokens. Children can buy prizes with their tokens whenever they have saved up enough.

THE BIG BONUS REWARD

But wait. Don't put away that list of Rewards yet. There's one more choice to be made. What if your child does a *perfect* job on the program for a *really* long time? Several weeks, or a month, or more? I think that this would call for a *Big* Bonus Reward. It might even call for a national holiday! You should not go into debt for such a Reward, but it ought to be worthy of the tremendous accomplishment that it will represent. The Big Bonus Reward is what your children, in their minds, will really be working for (although most children, of all ages, immediately start saving to buy a new car). It will help to pull them through the hard times as a shimmering beacon of future success. You should make it a good one.

The number of perfect weeks required to get the Big Bonus Reward should be realistically set for your child. This Reward should be attainable, but it should also be a genuinely big deal for children to get it. After all, it's a *Big* Bonus! Most parents of younger kids use three weeks or a month. Older children are generally required to go four, six, or eight weeks. Bryan's parents choose one month. (Between you and me, kids don't have to be 100% perfect to get the Big Bonus Reward, but *they* are not to be told that. We'll discuss it in Chapter 5.)

Bryan is completely taken with the Lego System, so his parents decide that the Big Bonus Reward will be one of the larger Lego sets, in the $20 to $30 range. They also decide to let him choose the particular set at the time that he is to receive the Reward. Bryan is thrilled with the entire Reward structure.

Your choice of a Big Bonus Reward should depend on your child's age and interests and on the depth of your pocketbook. Parents have successfully used such things as increased telephone privileges or actual telephones, health club memberships, a variety of construction or electronics kits, purchases of video games or videocassettes, small pets, toys, clothing, trips, parties, and cash.

There are several items that you should *not* use as Rewards, Bonus Rewards, or Big Bonus Rewards. Sleep-overs are a good example. If you use sleep-overs as a Bonus Reward, you must be prepared to have some strange, neighborhood kid staying in your house and eating your food each time your child has a perfect week. Week after week. On the plus side, this might serve to make your own children look that much more attractive to you. You might be thinking that a perfect week will be so rare that you'll be able to tolerate the few times that this will happen. Careful! It will happen more often than you think. Sleep-overs might serve better as Big Bonus Rewards.

I discourage parents from using visits to important relatives in the Reward system. A child should not be completely cut off from necessary social interactions as a result of behavioral problems. I also ask parents not to use reading to their children as a Reward, since kids should be read to as much as possible whether they behave well or not. Stay away from anything that is critical to your child's well-being and development and look for those optional, extra Rewards that will be special.

There are a number of important reasons for designing this three-level Reward system, and we will examine them in Chapter 5. For now, it's time to look at the last list.

BRYAN'S PENALTIES

David and Kathy come up with only four items for their Penalties list: time alone, no television, no video games, and no playtime with friends. This is usually the hardest list to construct, a fact that often comes as a surprise to parents who have spent large parts of their lives threatening to use a wide variety of gruesome punishments. A good Penalty is actually hard to find. Especially since we have *absolutely ruled out physical punishment.*

Although physical punishment can certainly bring about changes in behavior, it has a number of unexpected and undesirable side effects that make it something to be avoided. For example, physical punishment can cause a child to develop fear of the punisher. Most parents do not relish having children who are afraid of them. Parents who use physical punishment often experience guilt for doing so. The punishment can lead a child to become aggressive, or, conversely, to become withdrawn and generally inhibited. Whatever else it may be, physical punishment is certainly a form of parental attention. Even though it is negative, kids may value such attention enough to seek it actively by misbehaving. Physical punishment, if successful in changing behavior, can lead the punisher to become increasingly more aggressive. Finally, this type of punishment doesn't tell a child anything about what positive behaviors might replace the negative ones.

The approach to influencing children's behavior that we are developing here makes it possible to avoid physical punishment and its unwanted side effects. If you have been using physical punishment up to this point, or if you have used it in the past, you will now be able to tell your children that those terrible days are finally over. This announcement has tremendous impact on kids, who will realize that you are meeting them more than halfway. They will become even more positively invested in this approach. We will discuss the timing of talking to children about this, and all other aspects of the program, in Chapter 5.

Which still leaves us with the problem of coming up with creative Penalties. After getting this far in the book, you've probably guessed that there are going to be some rules to follow. The best Penalties are those to which you can add, or from which you can subtract. To spare you the agony of trying to figure out what I could possibly mean by that, let me say that ideal Penalties involve time subtracted from a favored activity. These would include such things as subtracting from time spent watching television, listening to the stereo, playing video games, or talking on the telephone. Time spent alone in a room, or time at home that might have been spent going out, are also penalizing to many children.

All four of the items on Bryan's Penalties list can involve time. I would discourage you from using restrictions in time with friends as a routine Penalty, however. This is another situation where a child's need for social interaction outweighs any possible benefit from restricting it. Even though I just used it as an example, don't send your kids to their rooms as the Penalty. We are going to use that one for something else later on. Penalties also shouldn't involve taking away the Rewards that your child has earned in this system, whether money, tokens, prizes, or something else. What's earned gets to be kept or spent, but it is never taken away. That leaves Bryan's parents with only two choices on their list of possible Penalties: subtraction of television or video game time.

You have suffered with me through the making of three lists, the operational definition of one list, and the refining of another list. You deserve a break on the Penalties, and I'm going to help you out. David and Kathy have an extremely powerful Penalty at their disposal, but they don't think to include it on their original list. It is by far the most effective Penalty for children from toddlerhood all the way to that blessed day when they finally leave your hallowed home (in their 20s, 30s, or, if things go terribly wrong, 40s), and it's simple. Send them to bed earlier than usual. This is usually experienced as a pretty heavy Penalty. The child is not allowed to be where the "action" in the house is. He or she also misses valuable time that could be spent reading, watching television, listening to the stereo, playing video games, playing with toys or siblings, or talking on the telephone. No kid (or psychologist) likes to go to bed early.

This Penalty also meets the condition that the time involved can be added or subtracted. We will be discussing why this is important in Chapter 5. That's where we will also decide how much earlier, and under what conditions, your child will be going to bed. For now, if your child would experience an early bedtime as a Penalty, then this is the Penalty to use. Bryan's parents decide to give it a try. For kids who don't care about bedtime (as if there actually *are* any), or for older children, restrictions in curfews as well as in telephone, television, video game, and stereo time are all effective Penalties. If you believe that your children won't be affected by any of these Penalties, see which of the items on your own Penalty list can be made to include a time factor.

I owe a large debt of gratitude to a family I worked with way back in 1983. Much of what I know about the penalizing nature of being removed from "where the action is" was learned from their six-year-old, very physically active son. This boy got completely out of control in my office, which, at that time, was an inner room with no windows. Neither his father (a policeman) nor his mother were doing anything to stop him. I told the boy that, if he continued his screaming and running around, I would throw him out. He didn't believe me. He should have believed me. Several minutes later, while still talking to his parents, I got out of my seat, grabbed his arm, opened the door, gently propelled him into the hall, and locked the door behind him. I briefly considered the possibility that his father might shoot me, but danger is all part of a day's work for . . . The Outlaw Psychologist!

The boy was now on the other side of the door. He was standing directly in front of a beautiful atrium garden and had complete access to a large physical rehabilitation facility with many easily available exits. What he then said has stuck in my mind ever since. As he banged on the door to my office, he screamed, "Let me *out* of here!" Let me *out* of here? *He* was out and *we* were in. What did this mean? I realized that he had been shut out from the center of the "action" that was important to his life, with his parents and me. This was penalizing no matter where he was physically. My observations over the years have confirmed that the bedtime Penalty works on this principle, as does the approach to time-outs that we will discuss in Chapter 5.

The Target Goals, Rewards, and Penalties are now complete. *You* deserve a Reward. Do something nice for yourself. Then turn the page and prepare to put this whole thing together.

*T*he Program

This is the point when parents often tell me that we've probably been wasting our time. This is also when I tell them that the parents I most enjoy working with are those who are initially skeptical, but who are also willing to give the program an honest try. I then get to look forward to the possibility of a future "I told you so" session. You have already put a great deal of effort into this project. The payoff is just around the corner.

THE GOOD STUFF

Let's use our old friend, Bryan, to explain how the whole thing works. Bryan's parents end up with twelve items on their final list of Target Goals. His weekly allowance is $5.25 a week, or 75¢ a day. The weekly Bonus Reward is either a small troll doll, Lego toy, videocassette rental, video game rental, or cash bonus of $2.50. The monthly Big Bonus Reward is a major Lego set. Finally, the Penalty is time subtracted from his bedtime (the amount of which is still to be determined) as well as other, unspecified Penalties too numerous and horrible to mention yet.

As soon as the lists are completed, I encourage Bryan's parents to start giving him information about the Target Goals and Rewards. I have already asked Bryan about the Rewards he wants, and I have let him know that I am working on a plan that might help him get them. I ask David and Kathy to give him more and more details as we continue our work on the program. At first, they are to drop little hints about the Rewards, always in a positive, light, and enthusiastic manner: "It look's like it's going to be an allowance, and you might get a raise. You'll have to do some stuff, but it sure looks easy. I don't know about this Schwarzchild guy . . ." (please feel free to leave out that last part).

In my office, I go over each Target Goal with Bryan and ask him which would be easy and which would be hard. Most kids tell me that they will all be easy. In this way, they help to convince themselves that the Rewards are attainable. Even when they are doubtful, however, the first Reward they receive will surely win them over.

Don't tell your child everything about the program at once. It's too much for anyone to digest in just one bite. You can always say that things are still being worked out and that you'll be giving more specifics as they become available. "We're talking about Legos, Bryan. Do you hear me? *Legos!*" Information about the Target Goals should be handled in the same way: "You're going to have to stop those insults when we ask you to do things. Shouldn't be too hard for $5.25 a week, though, don't you think?" "Wash your face, brush your teeth, get dressed, eat breakfast, clean your room, and be ready to leave the house at 8:10? You're already doing most of that, aren't you?" "Can you really do this for four weeks to get a Lego set? Are you sure?" And so forth. "Putting away items from one activity before starting another, hmmm? *That's* the one *I* think you'll have trouble with." Most kids will rise to this kind of challenge if it's issued in a friendly, humorous way.

At this point, the one thing that you should *not* be providing details about is the Penalties. The idea here is to generate enthusiasm in the child through your own enthusiasm. Part of your job is to be a good salesperson. You want your child to invest his or her energy in this approach even if you have some skepticism. I always encourage parents to be cautiously optimistic about the program between themselves and totally committed to it in front of their children.

The fact that there will be some Penalties should certainly be mentioned, but it should be minimized in favor of focusing on how well the child is going to do. You should always let your children know as soon as possible that physical punishment will no longer be used. The kids should be given complete information about the Penalties several days before the program starts or before the trial run (see Chapter 6, "The Chart"). I like to tell them that by doing not much more than they're already doing, they're going to make out like bandits. Later, I let them know that if they blow it, there's going to be a disaster.

Before the program starts in earnest, I encourage parents to declare a general amnesty and remove all punishments that are currently in place. No matter what kind of awful behaviors have resulted in the present state of affairs, I believe that the benefits of beginning with a clean slate far outweigh the costs. Eliminating the previous penalties acknowledges that the old approach wasn't working for anyone. It indicates a sense of parental optimism about the child's "turning over a new leaf." Kids appreciate their parents' flexibility and become more willing to make concessions themselves. Most importantly, having the burden of punishment for past behavior removed is immediately rewarding to children. Their investment in the new approach is increased right from the start.

If you *really* want to get your kids to support this program, you should point out that their biggest Reward will be the fact that you won't be nagging them anymore! Unless prompts have been designed into the system (as discussed in Chapter 6), the kids will sink or swim without having to worry about being pestered by their parents. They will get no reminders from you, since they will either take care of business and be rewarded, or miss Target Goals and be penalized. This idea is genuinely rewarding to most children. It is sometimes enough, by itself, to bring about miraculous improvements in behavior. The funny thing to me is that kids generally don't understand that being able to stop nagging is a parent's eternal dream. They think that we enjoy it!

And how does this program actually work? This is what you've been waiting for. Here's how it goes. Bryan has twelve items on his final Target Goals list. Each day that he successfully completes *all twelve items,* he receives his daily allowance of 75¢. *Only* perfect performance gets the Reward. If your list includes a Nighttime Package, the daily Reward is not provided until your child is actually in bed. It is usually best to give the Reward at bedtime, the end of the child's "workday."

Saving the Reward until the kids are tucked in is also a great way to encourage them to get to bed promptly. Since Bryan's Nighttime Package, Target Goal #3, includes his not getting out of bed repeatedly once he is there, it is decided that his daily Rewards will be given the following morning. There is an alternative to this schedule, which will be discussed later in this chapter.

For younger children, the giving of the Reward can be treated as an informal "ceremony." In order to reinforce the idea of parental unity and interchangeability, both parents should be involved in the ceremony or they should take turns providing the Reward when this is possible. Generous amounts of praise and fun should be provided. Although older children will probably just want to "take the money and run," some expression of parental pride is in order here as well. Kids generally respond to praise. In any event, *you must have the daily Reward on hand for presentation at the agreed upon time.* I believe that I may have mentioned this previously. No IOUs, and no excuses.

Your list of Target Goals is likely to include several items that your child doesn't have to take care of every day. Such things as weekly room cleanings, lawn mowings, and laundry stashings (on specific days and by specific times, of course) leave several days on which the target behavior is not required of the child. These are "freebies." Children get credit on the off-days when they don't have to take care of particular Target Goals. These Goals are treated as if they had been successfully completed. What a deal!

Kids also get freebies when items on the Target Goals list don't come up on a given day. Bryan, for example, gets freebies on every day that: he doesn't have to respond to his parents (Target Goal #2); he doesn't do anything wrong, get caught at it, or lie about it when he's caught (Target Goal #4); he doesn't have homework (Target Goal #5); the garbage doesn't quite make it to the top of the can (Target Goal #11); and the Three-Time Rule isn't used or taken to the limit (Target Goal #12). He will thus get the credit or the blame for each of his 12 Target Goals on every day that the program is running, even when some of the Goals don't require him to do anything. In "selling" the program to your children, you should point out these freebies and explain how they will make getting the Rewards that much easier. Kids are less overwhelmed by the total number of daily Goals when they realize that they seldom have to take care of them all on a given day.

So, Bryan has had his first perfect week. Perfect performance on twelve items for seven days. Eighty-four little victories. Who would have thought it possible? (I told you so!) He has qualified for the Bonus Reward, which he should receive on the day following the completion of his perfect week. This is the best reason for starting the program on a Saturday or Sunday. That way, the week will end on Friday or Saturday and the Bonus Reward can be presented on Saturday or Sunday. With this schedule, kids get some free weekend time in which to enjoy their earnings. The Bonus Reward is given on the first day of the next program cycle, even if there are problems on that day.

Time marches on. The perfect days turn into perfect weeks, which in turn become a perfect month. It's a miracle! Well, in fact, this would be a miracle. If you really get a month, six weeks, or two months of *totally* perfect performance, you should immediately suspect that your child has been taken prisoner by aliens from outer space. They have obviously substituted an overachieving look-alike to allay your suspicions while they 1) study, 2) exhibit, or, most likely, 3) become frustrated and give up trying to discipline your offspring. "But," I hear you say, "If even Dr. S. says that this much perfect performance is impossible, how will Bryan ever get his Big Bonus Reward? Is this some kind of cruel trick? Has Bryan been had?" Not at all. Perfection is too much to ask of anyone, especially if that anyone is a child. This is the one point in our system where there is some built-in flexibility.

I ask Kathy and David to decide in advance how many errors they would accept from Bryan each week before he would lose his Big Bonus Reward. They are comfortable with one or two misses. I tell them that errors in the first week of a monthly cycle are *always* fatal to the Big Bonus. Bryan would have to start from scratch, waiting for the next week of the program to again start putting together his four, "perfect" weeks (although he could still earn his daily Rewards). One or two errors in the second, third, or, especially, the fourth week, however, *might* be treated somewhat differently.

The further along toward the Big Bonus that children get, the more devastating it is to them if they lose it. The idea here is to keep them working toward a substantial goal, not to torture them with failures. If they make a mistake *after* the first week, they will usually complain or ask about losing the Big Bonus Reward.

I tell Bryan's parents that if, in their opinion, Bryan is generally doing well with the system, they might say something like this: "Look, you've been doing a great job. Keep up the good work and we'll *think* about getting you the Lego set anyway. We're not *promising* anything. But you've got to get back on track and do a great job from now until the end of the four weeks. *And don't tell Dr. Schwarzchild."* (I've actually had good luck with asking parents to "undermine" me in this way. An alliance is created between parents and children, with the parents replacing me as the ultimate authority regarding discipline in their household.) Remember that you are not to tell your children about this leeway in the Big Bonus Reward. That's between you and me. The kids need to strive for perfect performance.

Parents who decide to use an allowance system often ask me whether they can insist that their children save some of the money that they earn. They can certainly insist, but I encourage them to encourage instead. I feel that the money children earn should largely be theirs to control, just like yours is. This experience, including the mistakes they'll make, will help them to develop responsibility in dealing with money. On the other hand, *you* certainly don't get a free ride. You're stuck with paying bills and taxes. Maybe you should specify that a small portion be saved, with the option of more being saved if the child so chooses. (Yes, this sometimes actually happens.) My standard recommendation is that the major share remain under the child's control. Your usual, parental rules for spending still apply, such as limits and restrictions on buying such things as candy, toys, and tactical nuclear weapons.

"But what if my child *doesn't* have a perfect day?" That, of course, brings us to the next section.

THE BAD STUFF

Time to talk about those nasty Penalties again. These are what put the teeth into this system and make it different from the other approaches that you may have tried. In graduate school, I was taught not to mix Rewards and Penalties in the same behavioral program. I have since learned, through my trial-and-error work with families, that the power of this program lies in exactly such a mixture. Brace yourselves. We're coming to the most technical part of the whole book.

Let's get back to Bryan. An earlier-than-usual bedtime is the Penalty his parents chose. That's really only one among four Penalties that are used in this system. The first Penalty involves the loss of part of his allowance. There are twelve items on Bryan's list of Target Goals. If he accomplishes all twelve on a given day, the 75¢ daily Reward is his to keep. If he misses even *one* item, he gets *no allowance at all* for that day. This program uses an all-or-nothing approach to the daily Reward, whether it is money or something else. Because of this, a child cannot decide that it's worth giving up a portion of the day's Reward in exchange for ignoring some of the Goals (as in, "It's worth losing just 7¢ to get to hit my sister.").

"Gee, if he misses one Goal and loses all of his daily allowance, what's to stop him from ignoring the rest of the Goals for that day? What if he won't do anything else right?" Great question! Here's another one: "What if my child decides that it's worth losing her whole day's allowance in exchange for being able to miss some of the Target Goals?" These situations are covered by the fourth Penalty, coming right up.

For Bryan, the second Penalty is that even *one* miss on any day means that he won't get his weekly Bonus Reward. No toy, no rental, no cash, no way. Along with the loss of his daily 75¢ Reward, this Penalty makes misbehavior that much more unattractive to him.

The third Penalty is the loss of Bryan's monthly Big Bonus Reward. His Big Bonus Reward calendar is also reset to the beginning on the first day of the next "program week." As discussed earlier, this is always the case if your child misses an item during the first week of a cycle. If he or she has accumulated one or more perfect weeks before making a mistake, you can say that you will put off your decision about the Big

Bonus Reward until you see how the rest of the program goes.

Early-to-bed is the fourth Penalty. This is where being able to add to, or subtract from, the Penalty becomes important. For Bryan, the Penalty is time subtracted from his usual bedtime. This approach can work only if the child has an established bedtime. In Target Goal #3, Bryan's bedtime had been set at 8:30 on school nights and 9:00 on weekends. If you want to use bedtime subtraction as a Penalty, but your child doesn't have a usual, fixed bedtime, you will need to set an artificial "Penalty Bedtime." This is the bedtime that will magically appear, and be subtracted from, when the child receives a Penalty. When there are no Penalties, your child goes to bed at the usual time. Is this getting too technical? Hold on. There's just a little bit more.

This is how it works. Bryan's parents decide that ten minutes should be subtracted from his bedtime for each Penalty. If he misses one Goal on a given day, in addition to immediately losing his daily, weekly, and (so far as he knows) monthly Rewards, he goes to bed ten minutes early. If he misses two Goals, he's already lost all those other Rewards, plus he now goes to bed *twenty* minutes early. Three Goals missed gets him *thirty* minutes, and so forth.

I've found that this type of additive Penalty prevents kids from intentionally ignoring other Goals on a day when they've already been given a Penalty. It also makes them much less likely to decide that it's worth giving up some of their potential Rewards in order to freely misbehave. In this case, they will not just be losing a Reward that isn't even theirs yet. There is always another possible Penalty in the background, even when all of the major Rewards have been lost. This "fail-safe mechanism" is one of the main factors that separates this approach from the more usual allowance systems.

Now that you see how the Penalty adds to itself, you should select an appropriate amount of Penalty time for your own child. It should be enough to be punitive, but not so much that several Penalties will cause the child to go to bed hours earlier. I've had good luck with ten to twenty minutes per Penalty for kids of all ages.

Here's the trickiest part. On the *next* day, if he has a perfect day, his bedtime is reset to what it was before the Penalties, 8:30 or 9:00 in Bryan's case. This happens no matter how many Goals he had previously missed. He would also get his 75¢ Reward for the perfect day (even though the Bonus and, possibly, Big Bonus Rewards would be gone). If things don't go quite that well and Bryan misses *more* Goals on that next day, the Penalty time for each missed Goal adds to that of the day before. If he missed two Goals on Monday (twenty minutes) and one Goal on Tuesday (ten minutes), then on Tuesday he will be going to bed (twenty + ten =) *thirty* minutes early. The earlier bedtime continues to add to itself *every day* until Bryan has a perfect day, at which time he goes to bed at his original time. This approach gives children the incentive to put together a perfect day, and to get back on track, as quickly as possible.

Parents often worry that the bedtime Penalty will just keep adding to itself forever if their child misses a Target Goal, gets furious, and totally ignores the rest of the day's Goals. It doesn't help when I tell them that their children could end up having to go to bed as soon as they wake up in the morning: A child might eventually have to be reset to the current day by crossing the International Date Line! In truth, this situation is very rare. The Penalties put "teeth" into the program, and your children will do their best to avoid them.

Although the Penalties are definitely instructive, this program is designed to emphasize, and be driven by, the Rewards. Indeed, the Rewards that you give should far outnumber the Penalties. If this is not the case, some redesign in your Target Goals or Rewards is called for, or your children will become discouraged. The program, and you, should accentuate the positive. When Target Goals are missed and Penalties are given, the child should be reminded that a daily Reward can still be earned tomorrow.

Bryan's program is more complicated than some (of course) because of Target Goal #3. He has that annoying problem of not staying in bed once he gets there. What if he has a perfect day in every other way except that he won't stay in bed? At that point, it's too late to subtract from his bedtime. It already came and went. No problem. His bedtime subtraction Penalty will take place the *next* night, no matter how well he does on the rest of the next day's Goals. If he won't stay in bed on Monday night, even with a perfect Tuesday he will have to go to bed ten minutes early and lose at least one of his 75¢ daily Rewards. Of course, if he has other misses during the day, that time will be added to the Penalty from the night before. Clear? Sure! You might want to reread this paragraph eighteen or nineteen times. I did!

The complications of the stay-in-bed Target Goal were too much for a family that came to see me recently. They decided to use an alternate approach to this situation. Like Bryan, their thirteen-year-old son had a Target Goal about not getting out of bed once he was tucked in. They decided to *start* each new "program day" at bedtime, with the stay-in-bed Target Goal as the first Goal of the new day. Whatever Target Goal was to take place right before the stay-in-bed item became the last one of the previous program day. The Reward for that previous day was given *before* the boy got into bed. A mistake on the stay-in-bed Goal then became part of the following day's program. Easy. In their approach, no Penalties slop over onto the next day. They are having success with their new twist, and I pass it along to you.

Here's another good example of how this approach to improving children's behavior has changed and developed over the years. As I was finishing the first draft of this book, toiling away back there in the last few chapters, something happened in my office that required me to race back here and tell you about it. A family described an unexpected situation, which came up in the first week they were running the program. When they described what they had done about it, I thought it sounded perfectly reasonable. The strange part was that this situation *should* have come up many times since I started working with families, but this was the first that I had heard of it.

One of their nine-year-old son's Target Goals was that he not immediately respond with "no" when they asked him a question. In the first week, when he missed on this item, he would continue responding "no" even when he was told that he had already been penalized. His parents would wait a bit and then give him another Penalty on the same Goal. This continued until he would finally stop.

I was stunned when I heard this. We had never discussed what to do if a child repeatedly and willfully missed the same Target Goal right after the first miss. Indeed, I confess that the possibility of this happening had never occurred to me. The family solved this problem by continuing to add the usual amount of Penalty time for each of the multiple misses. It did the trick. How could this not have come up before? This Target Goal, and others very much like it, had appeared in dozens of these programs. It just wasn't possible that no child had ever continued challenging his or her parents after receiving a Penalty.

The answer slowly dawned on me. It became obvious that, when necessary, parents had routinely been giving more than one Penalty on a repeatedly missed Goal. It's just that nobody had told *me* about it. Oh, well. Nothing personal, I'm sure. Probably just an oversight. Hmmm.

In any event, you can take this same approach if you have a Target Goal that allows for repeated misses. You should let a judged-by-the-seat-of-your-pants-but-just-right amount of time go by between each miss, however. Although the total Penalty time for these misses will certainly be instructive to the child, a real power struggle here could result in too severe a Penalty. You might be able to interrupt the cycle with a Time-Out (to be discussed next) if your child will respond to it in the heat of battle. So, after all these years, this approach continues to evolve.

Here's another very recent addition to the program. I've been working with a fifteen-year-old boy whose parents are using a Home/School Homework Log in order to improve his academic performance. On his second day of using the Log, he forgot to get one of his teacher's initials. Realizing that this single omission meant that he would already be receiving a Penalty on his homework Goal, he decided that there was no reason to get any of his other teachers' initials on that day. Oops! His parents, who desperately want to be kept informed about all of his assignments, were understandably upset by this unforeseen turn of events. Our solution is similar to that for repeated misses on a single Goal. The boy loses his daily allowance and suffers an earlier bed time for the first set of missed initials, and an additional bed time Penalty is assessed for every other set of initials that doesn't appear. This change seems to be doing the trick.

TIME-OUT

"Time-Out" originally stood for "time-out from positive reinforcement." When negative behaviors took place, the child was sent to a room where there was essentially nothing to play with, nothing to do, and nothing that was at all stimulating. This was done to reinforce the idea that the good stuff was available only to kids who behaved. The bathroom was often the chamber of choice for Time-Outs (despite the fact that many adults, myself included, have a positive experience of the bathroom as the only island of peace, privacy, and reading in an otherwise uncontrollable world). It should come as no great surprise that I use Time-Outs in a somewhat different way.

In this program, a Time-Out is *not* a punishment. The Penalties have already been put in place. A Time-Out, for us, is the one tool that we can use to help our children avoid a Penalty. Once an item has become a Target Goal, you should not prompt your child to take care of that goal (unless this has been built into the system, as will be discussed in Chapter 6). Either it will be done, and the child will receive the Rewards, or it won't, and the child will experience the Penalties.

Time-Outs are to be used in situations where tempers are beginning to flare, and further developments will likely lead the child to violate a Target Goal. They are designed to interrupt a disaster-in-the-making. In a disagreement with his parents, for example, Bryan could easily get into trouble on Target Goal #1, "Bryan will not insult his parents when they have told him to start or stop doing something." At the point where the argument *threatens* to escalate into dangerous territory, Kathy or David should call a Time-Out. Once Bryan actually hurls an insult, it is too late for a Time-Out and a Penalty must be given.

A Time-Out is a fixed period of time when the child is to be in his or her room or in some relatively remote, previously designated area. You do *not* have to empty the room of attractive items, although you should insist that televisions, radios, video games, tapes, and similar items not be used during a Time-Out. The idea is to give the child time to calm down and refocus on the program. Activities such as reading are perfectly all right. As with the bedtime Penalty discussed in Chapter 4, it is removing a child from "where the action is" that makes a Time-Out effective. You don't have to create a "time-out from positive reinforcement" by making the poor kid do penance in the bathroom.

For the basic Time-Out, you should choose a period of time that is usually sufficient for your child to calm down.

Most parents find that between five and fifteen minutes is about right. If the child has gotten it all together after a Time-Out, it's back to business as usual. If not, another Time-Out of the same duration is called. This process should continue until peace again reigns in the household. Time-Outs should never be shortened for good behavior. Children should always complete each entire Time-Out without asking when it will be over. A timer with a signal that can easily be heard by all will eliminate the need, if not the desire, for whining. It is very important for you to explain Time-Outs to the kids before you start the program. Emphasis should be placed on the idea that this is *not* a punishment, but is designed to protect the child from Penalties. You're on *their* side!

Pop Quiz

What happens if you call a Time-Out and your child refuses to go? Don't read any further until you come up with a good answer. You have all the necessary information to handle this situation and many others like it. Hey, you weren't even supposed to read that last sentence before coming up with an answer. If you did, stop *here* and see what you can come up with.

For those of you who stopped, welcome back. For those of you who read straight through, shame on you. You have one more chance to figure it out before I give the answer. Here's a hint. How many chances did I just give you? Three? And if you call a Time-Out and your child doesn't go, what should you do? Those of you who said that you should use the Three-Time Rule are right on target and may consider yourselves deputized as Junior Psychologists, First Class. The Three-Time Rule was invented for exactly this type of situation. It allows you to deal with behaviors that are not usual and, therefore, are not included in the Target Goals. They become instant, temporary Goals. "Bryan, this is the Three-

Time Rule. I've just called a Time-Out. This is the first time I'm telling you to please go to your room." Now there are *real* consequences for refusing the Time-Out.

Congratulations! You have now completed the major part of designing the program. At this point, you should tell your child everything about it: Target Goals, Rewards, Penalties, Time-Outs, and the way they will all work together. Do an especially good job of explaining how the Penalty adds to itself for each missed Goal and continues to do so until there's a perfect day. Frequent repetition, along with your support and enthusiasm, will increase your child's investment in the system. As always, accentuate the positive while occasionally reminding about the negative.

CHAPTER 6

The Chart

The backbone of this entire approach to helping children behave is the Chart that you are about to design and construct.
Yes, it's time for chart construction. Truly one of the great joys
of modern parenthood. I'll try to make this one fun. Once you
see how the Chart works, I'll give you the rest of the details
about running the program.

DESIGN AND CONSTRUCTION

All of the Target Goals are listed on the Chart in language that
is clear to the child. Surprise! After suffering through those
nasty operational definitions, you now have to translate the
items into "kidspeak." Children of reading age should be able
to understand each item as it is written. For younger children,
the language should be easily understood when it is read to
them.

      The Chart also includes the days of the week and a grid
on which you will keep track of your child's progress. This
grid consists of boxes that will be marked to show whether
or not each Target Goal was accomplished on each day. It is
used for *one week only,* at which time you will start again
with a fresh grid (more on this shortly). Although you may set
it up any way you wish, most parents make a column of the
Target Goals on the left side of the Chart and put the days of
the week across the top. Bryan's Chart might look something
like the example in Figure 1.

FIGURE 1. BRYAN'S CHART

1. Bryan will not insult his parents when they have told him to start or stop doing something.

2. He will respond clearly and loudly, within five seconds, when his parents ask him something.

3. Bryan will take a bath, brush his teeth, pick a book, go to the bathroom, and be in bed with lights out by 8:30 on school nights and 9:00 on weekends.

4. Bryan will not lie when he is caught doing something wrong.

5. Bryan will do his homework each night at 5:30, and before 6:00 on Sunday. He will turn in assignments and show us his Log everyday.

6. He will take care of grooming and hygiene, get dressed, eat, clean his room, and be ready to go by 8:10 A.M. on school days, noon otherwise.

7. Bryan will receive no notes from school about wandering around the classroom at the wrong times, distracting other students, or fighting.

8. Bryan will put away items from one activity before starting another.

9. No more tantrums. Bryan will not scream, insult, hit, kick, or throw things when he is angry.

10. No hitting.

11. Bryan will take out the garbage when it is even with the top of the can, take his dishes to the sink, feed the dogs, and put his laundry away.

12. The Three-Time Rule.

	Sun.	Mon.	Tues.	Wed.	Thurs.	Fri.	Sat.

On Bryan's Chart, and on yours, each Target Goal should be fully written out. The Goals have been abbreviated in Figure 1 for illustration only. If all of the individual tasks in combined Goals (such as the Morning or Nighttime Packages) won't fit in the available space, use a simple name for the Goal (for example, "Morning Package") and attach a complete list of the actual responsibilities to the bottom of the Chart.

This is a chance to really let your creativity flow. The Chart can be constructed by mom, dad, one or more children, or any combination of family members. Think of this undertaking as one of those wholesome family projects that might get your kids away from the television for a little while. I always recommend that, when making the Chart, parents include the child for whom the program has been designed. This is another way to increase that child's investment in the system.

You should "shoot for the moon" in constructing the Chart. Younger children like things that are BIG, and I think that the Chart should reflect this. Make it as big as you can. It should be as gaudy and colorful as the child's age will allow. It can also be simple and tasteful, but it should always be something that will appeal to the kids first and the grown-ups second. Some parents put weeks into Chart design (too much), and some dash them off the night before (definitely too little). Let your own style be your guide and do it your way, as long as it works for the child. Young kids enjoy brightly decorated Charts, middle kids like decorated "theme" Charts (sports, horses, etc.), and older kids want things straight and to the point (plain forms or computer printouts).

The idea is to graphically show which Target Goals have been accomplished and which have not. A quick look at the Chart should tell both child and parents how things are going for the day and for the week. At the end of each program day, there should be something in every one of that day's boxes. Different colored marks or markers can serve this purpose, such as green for "got it" and red for "wrong." You need to display both the successes *and* the failures on the Chart for it to be effective. Although both should be recorded as soon as possible after they have occurred, it is especially important that the misses be indicated quickly. Children should be told that they have received a Penalty right after they have missed a Target Goal, or at the point where their parents become aware of the miss.

If you are using a paper or cardboard Chart, *make sure that marking on it during the first week doesn't ruin it.* Why the italics? Several years ago, I was presented with a beautifully designed and decorated cardboard Chart. The business part of the Chart, the grid itself, was nicely drawn at the center. Green ink marks filled all the boxes after the first week of the program (of course they did). Unfortunately, the parents hadn't realized that the same Chart would be used for the second week, the third week, and all the rest of the weeks. There was no way to erase the marks! This sad situation was relieved by pasting a new form over the old one, but it was never the same. You should also keep in mind that the Target Goals written on the Chart might need to be changed in the future.

A good approach to marking the grid on your Chart is to use two different colors or kinds of removable stickers. Labels made from adhesive reminder notes also work well. Cut them into interesting shapes if they don't come that way. At the end of the week, you can easily remove all the markers and be ready to start again.

Some folks have used a cork board with different colored pushpins or thumb tacks, or a flannel board with fabric markers. One boy's mother designed a flannel board that used a different sports item for each day's markers. For every Goal accomplished, he got footballs on Monday, hockey pucks on Tuesday, basketballs on Wednesday, and so forth. A missed item always got a referee. You can also use a piece of wood with hooks attached. Washers painted red on one side and green on the other can hang on the hooks as markers.

It took me a while to get one father to admit that he had spent hours at a drafting table designing his Chart. It looked like something that would have been at home hanging from the center of the ceiling at Madison Square Garden. All it needed was electric lights and a loud buzzer. It was truly a thing of beauty, and it included an idea that I have since recommended to everyone. His Chart had a space to record the number of perfect weeks that his daughter had put together. The child was able to see how far she had come and how far she had to go toward her monthly Big Bonus Reward. Good idea! Whether you choose to do it this way or not, don't forget to keep track of those perfect weeks. _That's_ a job that should be a pleasure.

Recently, a father who worked in the maintenance division of a general hospital had his _staff_ build a really beautiful Chart (I don't know if this sort of thing has contributed to the breakdown of the American healthcare system, but confidentiality will keep him safe). His design included a new and wonderful idea. He had installed a shelf at the bottom of the plywood board that supported his cardboard Chart. On this shelf, across the entire width of the Chart, was a clear plastic box divided into eight smaller compartments. Seven of these compartments, each of which had a separate cover and a tiny padlock, were at the bottom of the seven day-of-the-week columns. His son's daily Reward was an allowance, one-seventh of which was kept in each of these compartments. The eighth compartment held the cash Bonus for a perfect week. His child could easily see what he was going to get if he did well. This was a highly motivating view. The locks were not there to protect the money, but served to add pomp and circumstance to the nightly and weekly Reward ceremonies. It also lent a game show flavor to the whole undertaking, and was a big hit.

The same dad came up with another idea that has since been used by many other parents. When a Target Goal was missed, he took the allowance money that his son would have gotten for that day and put it in a glass jar. This jar was kept on top of the refrigerator and was labeled "For mom and dad." The visible presence of the boy's lost allowance served as another, powerful incentive toward good behavior.

The Chart should be mounted where it can easily be seen, several times throughout the day, by children and parents. The refrigerator door or kitchen wall is a possible choice, but I think that this is too public. It's important for your child to be frequently reminded of his or her progress. This information shouldn't necessarily be shared with the entire neighborhood or become a full-time, family preoccupation. The child's room or a family room may be the best location.

RUNNING THE PROGRAM

Here are some more details about the daily operation of this program. Be sure to review *everything* with your child one more time right before you start it.

In Chapter 5, we discussed when the Rewards and Penalties should be given. We also considered starting the program on a day that would allow you to give the weekly Bonus Reward during the weekend. What if you have to kill several days between the time you finish designing the program and the time you actually begin it? Here's an idea that works so well that you might consider using it even if you don't need to mark time before starting. You can run the program for a few days, or even a week, on a trial basis. I suggest that the Rewards be given during this period, but no Penalties. If Target Goals are missed during the trial run, your child should be told that there *will* be a Penalty for such misses when the program starts "for real." In this way, the child (and the rest of the family) has some time to practice and get the hang of the new system. The Rewards that you give during this time will get things rolling in a very positive manner. The trial run also gives you a chance to "fine-tune" the program.

In my practice, I usually see the child (or children) and parents together after the first week that the program has been running. This serves two purposes. First, I get to have my "I told you so" session. After having dealt with skeptical parents for several weeks, I welcome the chance to share in the joy that families experience with the successful start of the program. Second, we use this session to do any necessary fine-tuning. No matter how much attention has been paid to the design and construction of this system, there are usually some adjustments that need to be made. This may be as simple as changing the language in a Target Goal, or it may involve replacing entire Goals, Rewards, or Penalties.

Since most of you will not be visiting my office, you will be doing the fine-tuning by yourselves. The rule of thumb is to make as few changes as possible. If something is really not going well after a week, however, take the time to fix it. Remember, if what you're doing isn't working after a fair trial, stop doing it and try something else. If you are a couple, you will be well aware of where fine-tuning might be needed after a full week of the communication that we will be discussing in the next section of this chapter.

Should you prompt your children to accomplish their Target Goals? Only if you have designed this into your system. Reminders can be helpful for young children or for those with attentional or neurological problems. You should specify a maximum number of prompts, either as a general rule for all of the Target Goals or in the descriptions of individual Target Goals. For example, a Target Goal about not interrupting at the dinner table might allow for one interruption and one parental prompt before a Penalty is assessed. Unless they have special needs, older children should be responsible for taking care of business without any prompting by their parents. You should point out to your children that the best Reward in this system is that you won't be nagging them anymore (see Chapter 5). They will either take care of their responsibilities or suffer the consequences. Don't do the crime if you can't do the time!

You should *never* prompt your children in order to help them avoid Penalties unless prompts have already been included in your program. As painful as it may be for parents to watch their children make mistakes, it is sometimes important that mistakes be made. In this system, a child learns from the Penalties as well as from the Rewards. I believe that the effectiveness of this program is primarily due to the combination of Rewards and Penalties. Time-Outs are the only tool that you should use to help your children avoid missing Target Goals.

Parents sometimes ask how they should punish misbehavior that is not included in the Goals. It is not appropriate to use Penalties from this system for problems that aren't listed on the Chart. In these cases, you are left to use the usual, old punishments: room restriction, loss of privileges, grounding, and so forth. If you are dealing with a behavior that happens infrequently, this type of discipline should be sufficient. If the problem becomes repetitive, you should consider adding it to the program as a new Target Goal.

There is always the question of how long the program should be used. This is a tough one because of the many things that can change while you are using it. The answer depends very much upon your child's behavior. For example, many children make the system so much a part of their daily lives that a more traditional, Reward-only approach will keep it going after positive behavior has been firmly established. The Penalties and the Chart can often be dropped after an extended period of success. If the child's behavior then deteriorates, the full program can easily be resumed.

There are some children who might always require outside help in controlling negative behaviors. These include, but are not limited to, kids with certain neurological, attentional, and personality problems. In these situations, there is no reason not to continue with the program for as long as the child is in the household. Adjustments can be made, as necessary, to reflect the child's changing age and needs. In any event, guard against ending the program prematurely even if the child has been very successful. Be sure that good habits are solidly entrenched before you make big changes.

Another frequent question comes from families with more than one child. Should the other kids be ignored, or should they somehow be included in the program? Brothers and sisters usually answer this question by themselves. I used to be amazed when they insisted upon having their own Charts. Initially, it didn't make sense to me that siblings would want to be part of a system that includes some pretty serious Penalties. I now understand that the other kids are attracted by both the Rewards and the special attention that they see going to the child for whom the program was originally designed.

If you have other children with behavioral difficulties, you should certainly design individual programs for them. Even when it is not strictly necessary, however, I usually encourage parents to make Charts for their other children as well. Kids who don't have behavioral problems can participate in the program if their Target Goals consist of household chores. *Everyone* enjoys the experience of success. Remember that the Rewards for children of different ages don't have to be equal, but they should be fair. Older children will have more responsibilities and, therefore, should get greater Rewards. An in-depth discussion of this fairness issue, and how to design behavioral programs for siblings, is included in Chapter 7.

COMMUNICATION

Here, at the very end of the chapter, is absolutely the most important part of this whole book. If you are part of a couple, the need for you to frequently and consistently communicate about the program with your partner cannot be overstressed. Without this critical element, there is no point in your designing or trying to implement the program at all. This fact has been repeatedly demonstrated through the trial and error process.

You *must* set aside a minimum of five or ten minutes, *every day*, to discuss *everything* that has taken place involving the Chart. For example, a parent who has been home with the children *must* tell the other parent what behavior problems occurred and how they were handled. Which Target Goals were missed? Were the Penalties given immediately? What was the child's reaction? Was the Three-Time Rule used appropriately? Is there anything in the program that's confusing to anyone? Are there loopholes that need to be closed? Are the Target Goals, Rewards, and Penalties working well, or are changes needed? Is there more fine-tuning to be done? Did any Time-Outs go well? Is there enough bread in the house for sandwiches tomorrow? Okay, maybe not that last one, but everything else.

Both parents must know everything about the Chart. This level of communication makes it impossible for children to manipulate their parents by exploiting the differences in the amount of information that each parent has (the old "But Mom said . . ." again). It also allows parents to prepare themselves for those awful situations that have been repeating forever, but which were somehow not included in the Target Goals. You know the situations I'm talking about. The ones where the same battle takes place after the child does the same thing wrong that was also done wrong yesterday, the day before, the week before, and the month before. The

ones where you invent a different punishment for the same
problem over and over and over again.

I always enjoy this part of working with parents. They
tell me about these situations. I smile. "This happened
today?" "Yes, it did." "This happened yesterday?" "Yes." "Last
week?" "Yes." "Last month?" "Yes, yes, yes! We give up! What
should we do?" "Well, if it happened today, yesterday, last
week, and last month, I'm sure that you talked for five or ten
minutes last night about what you're going to do the next
time it happens." Silence. "You know that it's going to happen
again, right?" Silence. "Wait, wait, wait. Do you mean to tell
me that, even though this keeps happening, you don't have a
plan ready for the next time?" Sheepish grins. Gotcha!

I'll admit that my glee might be a bit childish, but this
is a trap that we *all* fall into, even psychologists who should
know better. It's just easier for me to see it from the comfortable distance of the therapist's chair than from the battle
zone itself. The daily communication period is an excellent
time to examine any repeating behavior problems that you
didn't list in the Target Goals. If they occur often enough, and
if there is no easier way to eliminate them, new Target Goals
should be written. This eliminates the necessity of dealing
with recurring problems as if they were new and having to
come up with those wonderful, spur-of-the-moment consequences ("You're grounded until the next time I see Halley's
Comet!"). The communication period is also when you
should determine whether Target Goals have outlived their
usefulness and are no longer appropriate or necessary. You
can then consider rewriting, dropping, or substituting more
relevant Goals for them.

I believe I may have mentioned that *the daily communication period is by far the most important part of this whole
program. Nothing else in the program will work if it is ignored. This level of communication must continue as long as
the program is running, every day, without fail.* The interaction

can be as simple as reporting that nothing relevant happened that day, but at least that much must be said. I would allow that, if one parent is on the road and the program has been well established, telephone calls for such communication might not be required every day. If the program is new, however, call every day.

Divorced parents who are running the same program in two households should communicate regularly about their progress and problems. Interestingly enough, single parents also need to have a daily communication period. These topics, and others which are related, will be addressed in Chapter 8.

What could possibly go wrong if the communication period is ignored? Here is a true and excellent example. I had designed a program with a couple and their thirteen-year-old son. It had been running for one week when the family came in for the fine-tuning session. "How's it been going?" I asked. "Pretty well," Mom replied. "A couple of times, I've had to tell him to get his clothes out of the living room before his father came home and gave him a Penalty. He's done it right away, though."

Dad's jaw almost hit the floor. You see, this was the first that he had heard about his wife's prompting. He remembered something about the system being designed to make parents equal and interchangeable to their children in matters of discipline (as mentioned in Chapters 1 and 4). "You aren't supposed to wait for me to come home to give a Penalty," he sputtered, "and you aren't supposed to prompt him about the things that are on the Chart!" He was right about this, of course, but he was also about to share in the criticism. "Gee," I said, using my most wholesome expletive, "wouldn't this have come up already if you two were actually communicating about the program every day?" Sheepish grins. This type of situation can be completely avoided if parents simply spend some time each day talking about the program. Again, candlelight and wine can be very useful accessories (ah, the romantic side of behavior improvement).

The communication period is the ideal time to discuss any questions or problems associated with the program. For example, your husband or wife has just used the Three-Time Rule for the fifth time during a single dinner. You believe (correctly) that this is at least four times too many. The appropriate response from you would be to: 1) scold your spouse until no one can remember why you're mad at the kids, 2) scream, 3) just give up and start crying, 4) send the kids to military school, or 5) none of the above. The correct answer is none of the above. No matter what kind of mistake your partner is in the midst of making, if there are children in the vicinity, your job is to bite your tongue and nod in agreement and support. Even if it kills you.

It is critically important that parents *never* undermine each other's discipline in front of the children. Remember, the idea of this system is to make parenting consistent and unified. This doesn't mean that you should always agree with what your spouse is doing (as if you could). My point is that you should discuss your disagreements later and in private. If parents then determine that a mistake has been made, they should go back to the child, explain their reasoning, and change the consequences. The powerful message that this delivers to children is that there is no shame in discovering an error and correcting it. As consistent and unified parents, you would certainly be together when you discussed the change with your child. Of course.

I may have put some emphasis on the idea that couples must communicate about this program in order for it to work. What if one partner is indifferent, lukewarm, or actually hostile toward this approach to helping your difficult child behave? If this is the case, then your work here is done. The ship of behavioral improvement is officially dead in the water. I appreciate all the reading that you've done up to this point, and I hope that you can put it to good use through consulting with the other parents in your neighborhood about how to improve *their* children's behavior. Unfortunately, this system will not be bringing about any positive changes in your own household.

Given that the mere lack of an ongoing communication period is enough to undo this system, an uncooperative partner in the house has the power to absolutely obliterate it. For this approach to be effective, two parents who are living together *must* cooperate in support of their children's best interests. Single parents will find useful information about running the program in Chapter 8, "Single Parents, Divorce, Ex-Partners, and Stepfamilies."

You now have all of the information you need to run your own program. Chapter 10, "Three Case Studies," will show you how some other folks did with theirs. If you run into major difficulties, please take a look at Chapter 11, "Troubleshooting."

CHAPTER 7

A Simple Allowance System, with Siblings

Wait! Don't skip this chapter just because your kids don't need a simple allowance system or because they don't have any brothers or sisters. There is information here that will be useful to you in designing a behavioral program no matter what your family situation is. Besides, one can never have too much practice in doing operational definitions, can one?

WHY ALLOWANCES FAIL

In the course of developing this approach to helping children behave, I've gotten to hear an awful lot about allowances. I'm always interested in what a child gets, and what he or she must do to get it. When a family and I decide to design a behavioral program, the allowance system that already exists in the household can provide a useful framework for further work. At the very least, it is a valuable source of information about how discipline has historically been applied in the household. I'm very glad to be able to report that allowances can provide this framework for further work and some helpful, historical information. That's because I can't figure out another explanation for why we all rely so heavily on them. They seldom seem to work.

    I believe that there are a number of reasons for the failure of allowances to get the job done. First, I've been surprised at the number of times parents give allowances to their children while expecting absolutely nothing in return. Many parents are willing and able to provide their kids with a steady, reliable source of income. I definitely agree that children should have money of their own to spend. I've always found that spending money is fun, and the kids with whom I work seem to agree. Having personal control of some cash also teaches them about the value of money. But not if it's given to them for free.

Through the hard lessons of jobs, mortgages, kids, and credit card bills, I believe that I've gained a fairly firm grasp of what is required to get and spend money. I have to admit that, having been a child who was given an allowance in exchange for doing practically nothing (oh, all right, Dad, it was actually for doing nothing), I didn't learn this until I went to work in the "real" world. Free money from the folks was certainly easier, but it always had strings attached to it. It's hard to develop a sense of independence when you are constantly begging your parents for cash, and then having to account to them why it disappeared so quickly. Money from working was harder, but it had more worth for being truly mine. Having to exchange some of my own time and energy for a paycheck made it that much more valuable.

If you are giving your kids free spending money and they are behaving well, don't change a thing. After all, "if it ain't broke, don't fix it." On the other hand, if your kids are behaving that well, what are you doing reading this book? (Please don't take this to mean that you should stop, of course. Perhaps you can be of some help to that neighbor with the unruly children.) If your kids are *not* behaving and you are giving them free spending money, it's time to consider changing the rules. As always, when you have given an approach a fair trial and it hasn't been working, you should stop it and try something else instead. Allowance systems can't be used to improve behavior if they are not directly attached to specific, parental expectations.

The second reason for the general failure of allowance systems is that, even when parents *do* have the expectation that certain responsibilities will be carried out before payday, the exact requirements for satisfying this expectation are seldom clearly spelled out. This lack of clarity can apply both to exactly which jobs should be done and to the instructions for doing them in such a way that parents will be satisfied with the results. "He knows what he's supposed to do for his money" is a phrase that has echoed through my office on any number of occasions over the years. I have learned that this doesn't necessarily mean that the child's idea of what is required matches that of the parents. Assumptions of this type have doomed many an allowance system.

Even when all of the participants have a similar view of which jobs are to be done, there is rarely any agreement as to what "done" actually means. I have noticed, for example, that my oldest son's idea of taking out the garbage differs somewhat from mine. (Caught in the act! Yes, it's possible that my own household may have been the model for The Great Garbage Pail Scenario, TGGPS, that I described so eloquently in Chapter 3.) We certainly agree about taking the bag from the small container inside the house to the larger containers outside the house. Where we part company is at my belief that there's a little bit more to that particular job description.

For example, when I next go to throw away that unusually wet and sloppy mass of paper towels that I've just used to mop up some really ugly, major spill (not necessarily, though quite frequently, related to this very same son), I'd be comforted to find that a new garbage bag has been placed in the can. I can actually count on its being there about once every other month. I also enjoy providing a minor challenge to our neighborhood dogs and raccoons by having the lids securely fastened to the outside garbage cans. Does it seem to you that this situation might be eased through the use of a well-defined Target Goal?

The third reason for the poor performance of almost all allowance systems is the aforementioned failure of many (a nice way of saying "most") parents to provide their children with payment in a timely fashion. It is my guess that more allowances have met their doom because of parents telling their kids, "If you wait until tomorrow, I'll pay you for both days," "I don't have any change right now," or "It will be better for you if I save up the change until I can give you bills" than from any other reason. There may be more of these cases than those in which the kids just didn't do what they were asked. And where did this idea of children's needing bills come from, anyway?

There is another, more abstract problem with late payment, and it is the basis for dividing the weekly allowance into smaller, daily shares. I have become convinced that many allowance systems fail because of the adult expectation that children can, and should, do a week's worth of tasks before getting paid. This is the model with which we're all most familiar. It's the way our allowances were given to us when we were kids, and, with the exception of those of us who must submit to a brutal, biweekly salary, it's the way that most of us are paid as grown-ups. The only difficulty here is that the younger the child, the less likely that this approach will work.

As we age, we increase in our ability to think abstractly. Jean Piaget, the French psychologist, found that this capacity is generally underdeveloped in children who are less than ten years old. Adults have no difficulty at all in understanding the idea that the hours they spend at work will later be transformed into paychecks. In fact, this concept is really quite abstract. While grown-ups can be motivated over a long period of time by a Reward that is not physically present, children require that things be much more immediate, concrete, and tangible. Even teenagers respond better when they don't have to wait too long for a payday. For us to ask our children to work toward a Reward that *might* come at the end of seven days could constitute cruel and unusual punishment.

In this case, the late payments are not due to an accidental mistake on the part of the parents, such as being caught without enough quarters. Rather, the allowance is *scheduled* to be given too late to reinforce a child's improving behavior. As you remember, in order to be most effective, a Reward should be given as soon as possible after the target behavior has been accomplished. To younger children, and even to many adolescents, seven days is an eternity to wait for anything. This over-delayed allowance creates a situation in which children can feel as if they are actually working for nothing. The possibility of exchanging work for the allowance is quickly perceived by the child to be unrealistic. Instead of creating a climate of challenge and expectation, the delayed allowance becomes a symbol for the unattainable and a constant reminder of failure. Needless to say, behavior seldom improves under these conditions.

Despite some accusations to the contrary, I do live in the real world. The ideal situation for behavioral change, wherein a Reward can be presented immediately after the target behavior takes place, generally doesn't exist outside of laboratories, circuses, and marine shows (I have some trouble with the image of your throwing a herring to the kids each time the garbage is taken out). In the real world, I believe that almost all children and parents are best-served when the Reward is given at the end of a single day. This period is short enough to be effective in improving the children's behavior, and long enough not to overly inconvenience the parents.

As with any rule, there are some exceptions to this one. If you are working with very young children, and if you have only a few Target Goals, a Reward that is provided right after the desired behavior occurs will be most effective. This approach needn't be too difficult, since younger children are frequently in the company of one or more of their parents. Similarly, children with significant cognitive or neurological deficits might derive more benefit from a program with immediate Rewards.

You can also make an exception in the opposite direction for teenagers who view the once-daily allowance as too childish. If these teens have developed enough maturity to delay their gratification for a week and still work for it, you might as well give it a try. You will simply have to do a little accounting of the Rewards and Penalties in order to determine the amount of allowance that is earned each week. Penalties, since they involve more than just the loss of the daily Reward, are always given right at the time that the infraction is discovered.

The last reason for the general failure of traditional allowances is that Rewards, alone, are often not enough to bring about real behavioral change. Many allowance-only systems work for a week or two before a child decides that the money is just not worth the required effort. It's generally not much of a problem for kids to give up Rewards that they never owned in the first place. As I mentioned in Chapter 5, it is the addition of the Penalties that gives allowances their power to change behavior.

Having now made a tremendous case for why allowances *don't* work, I again want to encourage you to consider using them whenever possible. As we discussed in Chapter 4, once children feel that money is personally valuable to them, there are excellent reasons to use it as a Reward. It is readily available (at least in small quantities), easily divisible, quite tangible, and widely appreciated throughout most of the world. Having to work for money gives kids an intimate understanding of its value. Most importantly, it tends to be the Reward that they want the most. I have noticed that many of us are willing to attempt even very difficult tasks when there is a reasonable chance that we will get something that we genuinely value in return. This appears to be true in jobs, love, video games, and life in general.

Through Bryan's unselfish participation, we were able to examine the construction of a behavioral program for a child with ADHD, an actual psychiatric diagnosis. I made the point that the approach detailed in this book is just as useful in constructing simple allowance systems for children who don't have major behavioral problems. It can provide parents with a consistent and unified framework for getting the kids to participate in appropriate household responsibilities. Children will benefit from the reliable source of income and praise that they get in exchange for taking care of their chores.

I also mentioned in Chapter 6 that brothers and sisters generally want to be included in these programs. In this chapter, we will go through all the steps necessary to design simple allowance systems for a new friend, Derek, and his two siblings, Patrick and Annie. As with Bryan, these kids are fictitious, but based on the real children with whom I have worked over the years.

Consider yourself warned: Here come a few more of those ever popular, always enjoyable, and much requested operational definitions for you to practice on. My apologies in advance.

DEREK, PATRICK, AND ANNIE

Derek is a fourteen-year-old, hypothetical child whose brother, ten-year-old Patrick, and sister, seven-year-old Annie, are hypothetical as well. (I can only be thankful for the abundant crop of hypothetical children this year. It just goes to show the importance of careful planting and soil conservation techniques.)

Derek is generally a well-behaved young man. Well, let's be honest. He is generally well-behaved for a kid of this frequently difficult age. Part man, part boy, his interest in girls is just starting to compete with his interest in animated cartoons. Video games and basketball are still tied for first place, however. His parents' complaints about him are relatively minor, but they have made very little progress in the few areas that are truly important to them. At the top of this list is Derek's poor school performance.

Although educational testing and past performance have convinced both his parents and teachers that Derek is completely capable of achieving average or better grades, he has displayed a steady decline in his academic scores over the past two or three years. Average grades have become his best, and he is now in danger of failing two of his ninth grade classes. Derek's interim school reports and report cards have become depressingly repetitive: "Incomplete assignments. Low test and quiz scores." There is no evidence, through either observation or formal testing, that he has a learning disability. My evaluation uncovers no major traumatic events, parenting difficulties, or conflicts that might account for the deterioration in his school performance. His parents, Tim and Linda, are generally unified in their approach to discipline. Derek displays no symptoms of significant psychiatric problems, but he has certainly become somewhat depressed about his parents' and teachers' school-related nagging.

Derek gets an allowance of $5.00 a week for baby-sitting his younger brother, emptying the dishwasher, doing his own laundry, and walking and grooming the dogs. He sometimes empties the dishwasher. He never walks or grooms the dogs. He always gets his allowance. (Hmmm. Something is definitely wrong here!) Lawn mowing, which actually does take place on an as-needed basis, is not included in Derek's allowance and is paid for separately ($10.00).

School performance is not included in the allowance, either. Tim and Linda have used monetary rewards on occasion and have had some success with them. They are not consistent in using this approach, however, so they end up with spotty islands of success in a sea of failure. Derek has learned the rules of this game very well (no one ever said he wasn't on the ball). He has become perfectly willing to lose the allowance money (that wasn't even his yet) in exchange for blowing off a marking period or two of French.

His parents' continuous nagging has become completely ineffective. There is essentially no meaningful, negative consequence for his doing poorly in school or ignoring his household responsibilities. Derek's allowance money flows into his wallet, week in and week out, without interruption (except, of course, when his folks don't have the right change in the house). This is a very good deal from his point of view but a very bad one from that of his parents and teachers. From my point of view, both parental consistency and a good Penalty are called for here.

Derek feels that his folks should *always* pay him for good grades, since both he and they know that this is the only approach that has ever worked. Something seems to be wrong here, as well. In Chapter 4, I used quite a bit of ink to convince you that using money for a Reward isn't really the same thing as bribery. Now, here I am saying that Derek not only understands it to be bribery but easily uses it for extortion. His attitude had become "No pay, no grades." No good.

I believe that this is an excellent example of how the use of a well-designed Penalty can prevent the failures that are so common with the usual allowance systems. In Derek's case, there is no reason for him *not* to try forcing his folks to cough up some cash. If he were also to run the risk of losing some of his video game privileges or other goodies in *addition* to not getting his allowance, the situation might appear very different to him.

Linda, Tim, and I decide that an allowance system, solidly based on the good old behavioral program, is the way to go in addressing these problems. Derek's previous experiences with an allowance show that, if nothing else, he is certainly interested in money. He tells us that cold, hard cash is still his most coveted Reward. The focus of the program will be to improve Derek's school performance and his participation in household responsibilities. There is no doubt that he is a really nice kid, but it is also obvious that there are some things that need to be tightened up just a bit.

"But what about the other kids?" asks Linda. Tim raises his eyebrows and nods in support. (I understand that we authors are supposed to throw in some descriptive scenes like this in order to create a mood.) When they hear that Derek is to get a new allowance, Patrick and Annie insist that they also be included. And why not? They are both already receiving allowances with very little expected of them in return, and each has a couple of minor, but annoying, behaviors that could easily be addressed through the program.

It turns out that Patrick is doing fine in school with the single exception of occasionally not getting all of his homework done. This has resulted in a number of those all-too-familiar, late night, crying/homework sessions: important assignments left undone are accidentally discovered by a highly annoyed Mom or Dad, and always after 9:00 P.M.

At home, Patrick is pretty good about feeding the dogs on his assigned days. His room, however, appears to have been hit by some type of reverse neutron bomb. You remember the neutron bomb, don't you? It was designed to get rid of people while leaving their buildings intact. The reverse bomb in Patrick's room had left the people alone while trashing everything else. Where could all that stuff have come from, and how did it get to where it was now? Hadn't the room just been cleaned up last night? What is this strange and amazing power of ten-year-old boys? Patrick receives $3.00 a week for his allowance. Like his brother, he is a genuinely nice kid.

That leaves seven-year-old Annie. She has to be reminded many times to put her clean clothes away, her room is generally a mess, and she seldom remembers to feed the dogs on her assigned nights unless she is prompted. Annie's temper tantrums, when she doesn't get her way, are becoming locally famous. Her current allowance is $2.00, rain or shine. She is also very nice.

So, we have three nice kids with some pretty run-of-the-mill problems. Tim, Linda, and I decide to design behavioral programs for all three at the same time. The work proceeds exactly as it had for our young friend, Bryan, starting with establishing the Target Goals and ending with fine-tuning the Chart. Most of our attention is focused on Derek's program, which is to be the largest and most important. I have always found that programs for generally well-behaved siblings are pretty easy to construct. They usually write themselves as you are working on the main project. We will go step-by-step for each child, as we would do in my office.

TARGET GOALS AND
OPERATIONAL DEFINITIONS

After I assign the three lists (remember the three lists?) to Tim and Linda as homework, they present me with their Target Goals for Derek:

1. He's got to do better in school. He should do his homework every night that it's assigned. He should study for tests and do school projects on time. Derek never reads anything that isn't about basketball or video games. We think that reading real books would help him in school, but he won't do it.

2. He will stop being a bully with his sister and brother. He teases them, and it sometimes gets physical.

3. Derek will stop leaving his stuff all over the house. This includes his clothes, bookbag, soda cans, food, and sports equipment.

4. His room is a mess. He never makes his bed, and he uses the floor for a hamper.

5. He will do his own laundry and put away his clean clothes.

6. It's Derek's job to walk the two dogs and brush the hairy one every day.

7. He should mow the lawn.

8. He should empty the dishwasher and take out the garbage.

9. Derek lies to us even when he's absolutely been caught doing something wrong.

A pretty typical list for a pretty typical kid. Patrick's Target Goals come next:

1. Patrick's room, desk, drawers, and closet are complete disasters. He needs to keep them clean.

2. He teases Annie too much. Of course, she teases him too much, too. ("We'll get to that part shortly," said the doctor, knowingly.)

3. He needs to do his homework every night.

4. If we see one more basketball card in the bathroom, living room, kitchen, or in any other room that's not his, he's not going to have to worry about any of these other Goals! He's got to put his stuff away when he's done with it. His outside toys think that they're _required_ to sleep under the stars.

5. Patrick is supposed to put his clean clothes away. We're supposed to win Lotto. There's about as much chance of one as the other.

6. It's his job to feed the dogs every other day, when Annie doesn't.

7. He should make his bed every day.

8. He should take care of the recycling on Friday.

Annie's Target Goals come last:

1. No more temper tantrums. No more yelling, stamping her feet, or screaming.
2. She's got to clean up her room and put away her clean clothes.
3. She teases Patrick as much as he teases her. The two of them can drive us crazy, especially in the car.
4. She has to take her turn feeding the dogs.
5. Annie is leaving more and more of her things around the house. Her outside toys are all over the place, too.

So, we have the lists of Target Goals for our three heroes. You can guess that this means we now have some operational definitions to take care of. Our work with Bryan has certainly prepared you to carry out this task with little interference from me. Before reading on, you might try your hand at figuring out the questions that Linda and Tim must answer in order to turn their lists into final Target Goals (hey, the practice will do you good).

Let's take a look as Linda, Tim, and Dr. Schwarzchild work on the operational definitions for Derek's nine Target Goals. Those of you who say there are *ten* Target Goals, because you remember that the Three-Time-Rule is always added to these behavioral programs as the last item, are getting somewhat ahead of things. You are, however, to be sincerely commended for devoting yourselves to this program at a level above and beyond the call of duty.

Derek's first goal is familiar to us from Bryan's original list of Target Goals. It's that old homework item. "He should do his homework every night that it's assigned. He should study for tests and do school projects on time." Tim and Linda decide to use the Home/School Homework Log described in Chapter 3. They set the time by which homework is to be done at 9:00 P.M. on school nights and on Sunday night. By choosing this approach, they allow Derek to have his all-important, after-school, wind-down, basketball/television session.

The Homework Log is set up with the school to include advance notice of tests and special assignments. As always, Derek is made completely responsible for presenting it to each teacher every day. We give special emphasis to the idea that teachers who are not assigning homework are to put their initials next to Derek's notation, "None." This is the most obvious loophole for him to try to exploit—head him off at the pass. Target Goal #1 becomes: "Derek will do his homework each school night and Sunday by 9:00 P.M. He will use and show us his Homework Log every day. The Log will include advance notice of tests." If he fails to have the Log initialed by his parents and teachers, or if he claims that he has forgotten to bring it home, he will receive a Penalty for that day.

Studying, Reading, and Practicing

It is worth noting that in our discussions of both Derek and Bryan, nothing has been said about a Target Goal for actually studying. It is certainly possible to add such an item, and you should definitely do so if your child's school performance would be helped by it. A Goal of this type would include the amount of time to be spent studying each day, what is to be studied, and when this studying is to take place. Parents *must* be available to directly observe their child in the act of studying, however, or said child might end up using the time for secret activities that are more personally satisfying (such as reading magazines, playing video games with the sound off, clipping toenails, or staring blankly out the window for hours at a time).

The actual studying for tests is probably best monitored on an ongoing basis rather than being left solely to the

Chart. If you are using a Homework Log, you will see the advance notice for tests when you are initialing it to show that each day's homework assignments have been completed. The most conservative approach is then to keep an eye on whether and when studying is taking place. A little encouragement is certainly in order. If your child rejects even your most heartfelt pleas, write a formal Target Goal about studying.

Tim and Linda decide that gentle persuasion is not going to be enough to get Derek to make good use of his study time. Instead of including an official Target Goal about studying, however, they discover a powerful approach, which we will discuss when we get to the Penalties.

Derek's folks are convinced that his lack of interest in reading anything of substance is a major factor in his poor school performance. This raises a number of questions about value judgments and generational differences, but I am comfortable with the idea that parents might want to ensure at least a minimal level of genuine literacy in their children. For Linda and Tim, this level requires that Derek go further than merely mastering the basic mechanics of reading and comprehending what he reads. They also want him to be exposed to the world of ideas, beyond the facts that the secret codes hidden in video games can improve his characters' scores and that professional basketball players make really huge salaries. He isn't required to dabble in Camus and Nietzsche, but Derek's folks hope to encourage him to explore a little more "who, what, when, where, how, and why" in his literary pursuits.

Parents frequently ask whether Target Goals about such things as reading can be included in this program. Musical instrument practice, sports, religious instruction, Boy or Girl Scouts, and other wholesome, after-school activities are often the lightning rods for conflict between children and their well-meaning parents. If it is something that is important to you, it can certainly be included on the Chart. I have heard rumors that sometimes children need to be dragged, kicking and screaming if necessary (metaphorically, of course), toward doing something that is initially distasteful, but that might be highly enjoyable or beneficial to them later on. Perhaps I, myself, was forced to take a certain number of tap dancing lessons in my youth. Now, there was a good investment! The tap dancing psychologist. Maybe this is not the best example. I really can't recall doing the least bit of tapping for the last several decades. In any event, these types of activities can easily be added to your program. It is always worthwhile discussing exactly what your child is objecting to, however.

Tim and Linda want Derek to read for a minimum of thirty minutes each day. This actually means that Derek will read for _exactly_ thirty minutes a day, since he can be counted on to avoid the potential tragedy of accidentally becoming over-educated. Since reading is being viewed as a school-related activity, we decide to include it in the first Target Goal despite the fact that it is expected to go on throughout the year. That will serve to make this Target Goal useful even during the summer.

Derek's parents are as realistic about what he might read when left to his own devices as they are about how he might study when free from their supervision. Therefore, Target Goal #1 is rewritten: "Derek will do his homework each school night and Sunday by 9:00 P.M. He will use and show us his Homework Log every day. The Log will include advance notice of tests. Derek will read material, chosen or approved by his parents, for a minimum of thirty minutes each day. He should expect to be observed, spot-checked, and/or quizzed frequently and regularly." Nice.

Derek's second Target Goal is another familiar one: "He will stop being a bully with his sister and brother. He teases them, and it sometimes gets physical." As you can imagine, teasing can truly be prevented only when a parent is actually around to see and hear it. Otherwise, you are left to sift through a lot of accusations about who was teasing whom and, of course, who started it. If you are not there to experience it, and unless the evidence against one of the kids is overwhelming, you should probably forget it. You'll have other chances to make the point.

When there seems to be habitual teasing going on behind your back, however, you may want to include an item saying that the offender will be considered guilty until proven innocent. You should only do this if the other kids can be trusted not to abuse the reporting privilege. There's always the chance that one child will unjustly accuse another of teasing just to get that annoying sibling in trouble. Not that any of *our* children would resort to such tricks, of course.

In my continuing quest for good operational definitions, I have found that teasing can best be dealt with when it is reduced to the single behavior of name-calling. This certainly doesn't capture the full richness of teasing that your average fourteen-year-old boy can unleash, but we are again looking for specific behaviors that can be seen or heard. It is surprisingly difficult to carry out good, high-level teasing if name-calling is prohibited.

Derek's folks and I redefine his bullying as refusing to take "no" for an answer from the other two kids. Target Goal #2 for Derek becomes: "He will not call his sister or brother names. When they tell him that they don't want to do something, he will accept it without asking them more than twice. He will not hit, kick, pinch, push, or throw them." The "asking them more than twice" phraseology is based on our feeling that any kid, when turned down after inviting the sibs to participate in some activity, should get at least one additional "Aw, c'mon, please?" As always, Linda and Tim are to be the final judges of whether or not teasing and bullying have taken place.

"Derek will stop leaving his stuff all over the house." Where have we seen this one before? I recommend the always fashionable Scattered Items Goal. Target Goal #3 becomes: "Derek will put away items from one activity before starting another. This includes his clothes, bookbag, soda cans, food, and sports equipment." Putting it this way saves so much time, energy, and detail work. All the individual objects that are left in all the wrong places can be dealt with at the same time. This is one of my favorite tools. Once again, special dispensation can be granted to kids who are involved in long-term projects. They might be allowed not to put away the items being used in these works-in-progress, but *only* with parental permission.

And now, the messy room. If you're tired of this one as a parent, imagine how I must feel as a psychologist. I don't deal with just one untidy child or a few sloppy brothers and sisters. I've gotten to hear about dozens and dozens of messy rooms. Day after day, year after year. And that doesn't even include my own kids' rooms. *Every* kid has a messy room. All right, all right. I know that's not entirely true, but that's the way it sometimes seems from the vantage point of my office.

Derek's Target Goal #4 borrows a bit from Bryan: "He will clean his room before leaving for school each morning and before noon on weekends and in the summer. Room cleaning means making the bed, picking up all items that don't belong on the floor, and putting dirty laundry in the hamper." I've found that many parts of these programs apply to a variety of children in different families, and I always feel comfortable in stealing language that has worked before. You should feel free to use any of the actual Goals that appear in this book if they apply to your family's needs.

In complete fairness to Derek, it must be said that he always does his own laundry on an as-needed basis. This started several months earlier with the onset of a more intense segment of his adolescence. Mom and Dad were asked to relinquish all claims to controlling Derek's clothing. Unbeknownst to Derek, this suited Mom and Dad just fine.

The only problem is the fact that unless he is forced to do otherwise, he does not think twice about leaving loads of laundry in the washer or the dryer for up to several weeks at a time. He clearly subscribes to Newton's Third Law of Laundry, which states that a load at rest tends to stay at rest unless acted upon by an angry parent. This attitude can easily cause Mom or Dad to get intimately involved with his clothing once again, since the rest of the family's laundry would become seriously backed up in the pipeline. It is even conceivable that an argument could ensue.

Tim and Linda decide to specify that Derek's laundry has to be done at least once each week. This is actually just a formality, since his laundry schedule is not really a problem. Target Goal #5 becomes: "He will do his laundry at least once weekly. Doing the laundry means that it will be removed from both the washer and dryer before 7:00 P.M." The starting and ending days for Derek's laundry week would be set at the time that the program was to start.

The next one is easy. Target Goal # 6 states, "It's Derek's job to walk the two dogs and brush the hairy one every day." Sharp-eyed readers should now be wondering whether this can possibly stand up as a good operational definition for the dog item. No! "It's Derek's job to walk the two dogs and brush the hairy one every day by *9:00 P.M.*" Now, *that's* an operational definition. This Goal will work together with the dog items on Patrick and Annie's Charts to bring about a previously unimaginable level of pet care. The kids will handle it, just like they said they would when you agreed to bring Fluffy, King, or that incredibly boring lizard ("It hasn't moved in days. Are you sure it's not dead?") home for them.

Up until now, Derek's lawn mowing has been a service for which his parents have contracted separately from his allowance. In Chapter 4, we discussed the idea that Rewards work best when the potential recipient is usually deprived of them. Therefore, Linda and Tim now decide to include lawn mowing in the behavioral program to prevent Derek from having an independent source of income within the family. Such money, if unrelated to his allowance system, would likely make the Rewards seem less important to him. Including it in the program serves the purpose of linking his lawn mowing money to the rest of his household and academic responsibilities. It is now included in the larger Reward that Derek can get only by taking care of *all* of his new Target Goals.

It should be noted that my emphasis on cutting off other sources of income applies only to money that comes from family members, however. It is my opinion that children who are old enough to work, who want to work, and who are actually working, should generally be cherished. Although that minimum wage, hamburger-flipping money that flows into your children's pockets may diminish the appeal of a monetary Reward at home, the benefits of their holding real jobs should never be discounted. Since I don't think that you'll be able to get away with attaching your teenagers' paychecks in support of this behavioral program, these wages should remain as separate income for them. It's been my experience that most kids value money enough to make it an effective Reward even when they hold outside jobs. If this is not the case in your household, you should consider using a non-monetary Reward, such as coupons or tokens, which are redeemable for privileges.

In summary, Target Goal #7 is written to say: "He will mow the lawn once weekly. This is to include weed whacking and putting away the tools." All Goals should be this easy to write! As with the laundry, the days on which the lawn mowing week are to start and stop will be set at the start of the program. Due to the tendency of grass to disappear during the winter months, it is decided that snow shoveling, carving ice sculptures, or some other seasonal chore will be substituted for lawn mowing when appropriate.

Target Goal #8, dish washing and garbage patrol, is also easy. Linda and Tim write: "He will empty the dishwasher, when it is filled with clean dishes, at least once daily by 6:00 P.M. He will also empty it upon parental request. He will then move any dirty dishes from the sink to the dishwasher." Since there's no use beating a dead TOTGC, we steal the rest from Bryan: "Derek will take out the garbage when it is even with the top of the can or upon a parent's request. Pushing the garbage down in the can is allowed *only* before his parents have noticed a violation."

Tim and Linda's next item deals with lying. As you recall, this was also a problem for Bryan's parents. In Chapter 3, I mentioned that we cannot eliminate behavior if we are not even sure that it is taking place. This makes it almost impossible to completely eliminate lying. The situation isn't totally hopeless, however, since you can at least decrease the amount of lying in your home. Goals relating to lying can address only the times when parents have actually *caught* their children lying. So Target Goal #9 becomes: "Derek will not lie when he has been caught doing something wrong. His parents will be the final judges as to whether he is lying."

That's it, right? Of *course* not. It's another one of those annoying little pop quizzes. This one should be a snap. What happens next? Is something missing here? What could it be? Why, it's the Three-Time Rule, of course. That becomes Target Goal #10.

Here is Derek's finished Target Goals list:

1. Derek will do his homework each school night and Sunday by 9:00 P.M. He will use and show us his Homework Log every day. The Log will include advance notice of tests. Derek will read material, chosen or approved by his parents, for a minimum of thirty minutes each day. He should expect to be observed, spot-checked, and/or quizzed frequently and regularly.

2. He will not call his sister or brother names. When they tell him that they don't want to do something, he will accept it without asking them more than twice. He will not hit, kick, pinch, push, or throw them.

3. Derek will put away items from one activity before starting another. This includes his clothes, bookbag, soda cans, food, and sports equipment.

4. He will clean his room before leaving for school each morning and before noon on weekends and in the summer. Room cleaning means making the bed, picking up all items that don't belong on the floor, and putting dirty laundry in the hamper.

5. He will do his laundry at least once weekly. Doing the laundry means that it will be removed from both the washer and dryer before 7:00 P.M.

6. It's Derek's job to walk the two dogs and brush the hairy one every day by 9:00 P.M.

7. He will mow the lawn once weekly. This is to include weed whacking and putting away the tools.

8. He will empty the dishwasher, when it is filled with clean dishes, at least once daily by 6:00 P.M. He will also empty it upon parental request. He will then move any dirty dishes from the sink to the dishwasher. Derek will take out the garbage when it is even with the top of the can or upon a parent's request. Pushing the garbage down in the can is allowed *only* before his parents have noticed a violation.

9. Derek will not lie when he has been caught doing something wrong. His parents will be the final judges as to whether he is lying.

10. The Three-Time Rule.

It's worth noting that Derek has a number of "freebies" on his Target Goals list. As you remember from Chapter 5, kids get credit for the off-days on which they don't have to take care of particular Target Goals or when those Goals don't come up. Children will feel less overwhelmed by the whole system when you point out how frequently their Rewards will be based on things that they actually don't have to do every day. Derek, for example, gets freebies for doing his laundry and mowing the lawn. These are once-weekly chores for which he will receive free Reward credit on the six other days when he doesn't have to do them. He also gets credit for any day on which he doesn't call the other kids names, leave his stuff around the house, lie (or get caught at it, anyway), or provoke his parents into penalizing him with the Three-Time Rule. Derek will be cheered and enthused when he realizes that his only daily Target Goals are homework, dog walking and grooming, room cleaning, and dishwasher/garbage emptying. He will see himself entering that new car showroom, putting his cash down payment on the salesman's desk, and driving off in that sparkling new Corvette. It works for him, and it works for you.

THE SIBS

Here comes the really easy part. Well, relatively easy, anyway. Patrick and Annie can certainly be a handful for their folks, either individually or as a pair. Their sometimes difficult behavior is not the reason that these programs are being designed, however. It is unlikely that Linda and Tim would have developed this type of formal allowance system without the inspiration of Derek's school problems. They choose to include the other children primarily to avoid jealousy. Even with this motivation, however, there is no reason for them not to work on improving the other two kids' mildly problematic behaviors. That is exactly what a simple allowance system is supposed to accomplish. Since there is less at stake in bringing about behavioral change for Patrick and Annie, their programs are that much easier to design and construct.

First, we'll work on Patrick's seven (or eight, if you're still getting ahead of me with the Three-Time Rule) Target Goals. The first item is about his messy room/desk/drawers/closets. Stealing liberally from his brother, we will make Target Goal #1, "He will clean his room before leaving for school each morning, and before noon on weekends and in the summer. Room cleaning means making the bed, picking up all items that don't belong on the floor, and putting dirty laundry in the hamper." Here we have the well-known story of the second child having little that is his alone, but inheriting the older sib's hand-me-downs. Patrick has even inherited his brother's fourth Target Goal. We'll make it more personal by adding, "This will include special attention to his desk, drawers, and closet."

Tim and Linda's next Goal, about Patrick's teasing of Annie, encourages more theft from Derek's list. Target Goal #2 becomes: "He will not call his sister or brother names. When they tell him that they don't want to do something, he will accept it without asking them more than twice. He will not hit, kick, pinch, push, or throw them." You can now clearly see why the design work for siblings is usually so much easier than for the child who is originally identified as having the most difficulty. Many of the items usually turn out to be either the same or quite similar. In this case, the parents decide not to restrict this Goal to Patrick's teasing of just Annie, but to leave it exactly as it was written for Derek. With the addition of a similar Goal for Annie, all of the name-calling and bullying among the siblings is covered.

Here comes that all-time favorite Target Goal, the homework item. Target Goal #3 also borrows a bit from Derek's list: "Patrick will do his homework each school night and Sunday by 9:00 P.M." Since his school problems are relatively minor, there is no need to use a Homework Log. Linda and Tim decide to make one addition that reflects Patrick's individual needs, however. In contrast to his brother's predominantly athletic and external orientation, Patrick might be characterized as artistic and internal. As a matter of fact, he might be called somewhat "spacey," a creative dreamer.

For this homework Goal, the couple allows for a single parental prompt to be given each day as a means of focusing Patrick's attention on the scholarly tasks at hand. It will be given in person or by telephone, with the parents taking responsibility for making this contact. Target Goal #3 is rewritten to say, "Patrick will do his homework each school night and Sunday by 9:00 P.M. His parents will remind him of this once, and only once, each day."

Unlike his older brother, Patrick genuinely enjoys reading. Given his tendency to spend huge amounts of time in drawing, writing, inventing, shooting baskets, or merely contemplating the nature of the bubbles in carbonated soft drinks, he sometimes forgets that he genuinely enjoys reading. His folks decide to make reading a formal part of Patrick's daily schedule by taking another leaf from Derek's book. The final version of Target Goal #3 becomes: "Patrick will do his homework each school night and Sunday by 9:00 P.M. His parents will remind him of this once, and only once, each day. He will read material, chosen or approved by his parents, for a minimum of thirty minutes each day." Since Patrick can be relied upon to carry out his reading assignments as single-mindedly as he pursues new basketball cards for his sprawling collection, there will be no need for observing, spot-checking, or quizzing him.

Tim and Linda, if they were real people, would surely want me to explain the seriousness of the basketball card problem that they mention in the fourth item. This assumption is based on any number of real situations that have been described, in painful detail, in my office. It can be sports cards, rocks, bottle caps, sea shells, or those little paper tabs at the end of the strings on tea bags (do they have their own name?), but it is always a collection of small items that are widely distributed throughout the house.

Efforts to contain the individual specimens are effective for an hour, at most, and only then if the child is completely distracted, asleep, out of town, or in the army. You would not believe the amount of office time that a couple like Tim and Linda can spend talking about "The Collection." Or about the toys spread across the lawn, garden, driveway, and neighbor's property. This can easily become the major theme in a couple's life.

Scattered items always call for the now-famous Scattered Items Goal, with any necessary emphasis added for the particular child in question. In Patrick's case, Target Goal #4 becomes: "He will put away items from one activity before starting another. This includes putting away his basketball cards, clothes, bookbag, soda cans, food, sports equipment, and outside toys, especially his basketball cards."

Next, we deal with Patrick's failure to put away his clean clothes. There is no official laundry schedule in the household, with two adults and the oldest child often competing for the necessary machinery on an as-needed basis. Although Derek's new time limit for finishing his laundry will ease this situation, there is no real way of knowing in advance exactly when fresh clothing for Patrick will show up. This goal has to be stated in such a fashion that Patrick will put away his clothes no matter when they appear. Target Goal #5 is written, "He will put away his clean clothes, when they are placed on his bed, by 9:00 P.M. on the day that they are placed there." A bit legalistic, perhaps, but quite effective.

By now, the operational definition of items about such things as feeding the dogs should be almost second nature to you. Target Goal #6 is "Patrick will feed the dogs every other day before leaving for school and before noon on weekends and in the summer." To avoid the inevitable arguments about whose day it is to take care of the feeding, Linda and Tim decide to keep track of the rotation between Patrick and Annie by appropriately marking the family's master calendar. The energy the couple would save by side-stepping this potential conflict area could be put to better use in such refreshing, fulfilling activities as garage and basement cleaning.

The seventh item on the list, bed making, was covered in the first Target Goal. Tim and Linda next decide to add a chore for Patrick. His new responsibility becomes Target Goal #7: "He will tie the recycling bag and take it to the curb before 12:00 noon on Fridays." The noon deadline here is an example of how a single time can work throughout the year, even when a child's schedule changes. During school, Patrick will have to take care of the recycling before he leaves the house in the morning. In the summer, it will have to be done before he goes to camp, or before noon if he is just hanging around the house and driving one or more of his parents crazy until school, blessedly, starts again.

Target Goal #8? The Three-Time Rule. It's universal.

That covers all of Patrick's items. In summary, here is his final list of Target Goals:

1. He will clean his room before leaving for school each morning, and before noon on weekends and in the summer. Room cleaning means making the bed, picking up all items that don't belong on the floor, and putting dirty laundry in the hamper. This will include special attention to his desk, drawers, and closet.

2. He will not call his sister or brother names. When they tell him that they don't want to do something, he will accept it without asking them more than twice. He will not hit, kick, pinch, push, or throw them.

3. Patrick will do his homework each school night and Sunday by 9:00 P.M. His parents will remind him of this once, and only once, each day. He will read material, chosen or approved by his parents, for a minimum of thirty minutes each day.

4. He will put away items from one activity before starting another. This includes puting away his basketball cards, clothes, bookbag, soda cans, food, sports equipment, and outside toys, especially his basketball cards.

5. He will put away his clean clothes, when they are placed on his bed, by 9:00 P.M. on the day that they are placed there.

6. Patrick will feed the dogs every other day before leaving for school and before noon on weekends and in the summer.

7. He will tie the recycling bag and take it to the curb before 12:00 noon on Fridays.

8. The Three-Time Rule.

Patrick gets freebies on any day that he has no clean clothes to put away, when it's Annie's turn to feed the dogs, and when there's no recycling. He also gets freebies when he doesn't call his brother or sister names, leave any of his stuff around, or bring about a Penalty under the Three-Time Rule.

Last comes little Annie, seven years of rompin', stompin', temper tantrumin' dynamite. Her disposition is generally good, right up to the point where she inevitably becomes tired, frustrated, and cross. Then, if she isn't getting her way, she accelerates from zero to sixty in no time at all. Her tantrums consist of crying, snorting, stamping, door slamming, and yelling "I don't care!" This is generally followed by her returning to normal after a short while and acting as though nothing had happened at all. Linda and Tim have had just about enough of this.

Their first item for Annie becomes Target Goal #1, "No more tantrums. This includes snorting, stamping, door slamming, and yelling." Since Annie's family is hypothetical, I can assume that they have already spent a good deal of time discussing the different ways that she can express her anger without getting into trouble on the Chart. If your family is not hypothetical, don't forget this important step when you include similar Goals in your program.

Next comes Annie's room and clean clothes, items that also appeared on her brothers' lists. This Goal has to be adjusted for her fledgling bed-making skills, however. Target Goal #2 is written to say "She will clean her room before leaving for school each morning and before noon on weekends and in the summer. Room cleaning means straightening the bed, picking up all items that don't belong on the floor, and putting dirty laundry in the hamper." Although Tim and Linda originally mention Annie's room and laundry in the same item, we decide to assign the clean clothes to Target Goal #3, "She will put away her clean clothes, when they are placed on her bed, by 9:00 P.M. on the day that they are placed there." Splitting the original item in two, and later adding a new item about general household chores, ultimately result in Annie and Patrick's having equal numbers of Target Goals. We will shortly discuss whether or not this is important.

Again, courtesy of her brothers, the teasing item is easy. Target Goal #4 becomes: "She will not call her brothers names. When they tell her that they don't want to do something, she will accept it without asking them more than twice. She will not hit, kick, pinch, push, or throw them." Patrick also provides us with Target Goal #5, the dog feeding item: "Annie will feed the dogs every other day before leaving for school and before noon on weekends and in the summer." We then borrow Derek and Patrick's Scattered Items Goal for Annie's Target Goal #6, "She will put away items from one activity before starting another."

Although Tim and Linda haven't listed any other Target Goals for Annie, we decide to add one more before getting to the Three-Time Rule. It seems like a good idea to have the same number of Goals for Annie and Patrick. This decision appears to run contrary to the opinion I expressed in Chapter 6, where I stated that Rewards for children of different ages don't have to be equal, but they should be fair. I believe that this holds for Penalties and Target Goals as well. It is very easy to confuse equality with fairness. Parents have the right to deal with each child as an individual, tailoring the behavioral expectations and related consequences to that particular child's needs and abilities. There is no requirement that siblings should all have the same number of Target Goals or the same levels of Rewards and Penalties. And yet now I'm saying that we should add a Goal to Annie's list in order to make it equal to Patrick's. What gives?

This is a case where making a small adjustment in advance can save a large amount of grief in the near future. You see, Annie and Patrick are extremely competitive with each other. There is no doubt that different numbers of Target Goals would result in mayhem. In this situation, Linda and Tim can make a minor, but highly positive, modification to the program well before the children are directly involved. This "preemptive strike" isn't the same as caving in to their children's endless badgering for equality once the program is constructed. Rather, these parents are free to choose whether they want to avoid a possible trouble spot while they are actually designing the system. There is also no particular reason not to give these two kids an equal number of Target Goals.

You certainly don't have to ignore a potential disaster if you can see it coming. On the other hand, if equalizing the number of Goals between your children distorts the program by requiring you to make too many additions and/or subtractions, then definitely don't do it. An unnecessary quest for equality is not sufficient reason for you to violate the integrity of your program. When the Target Goals, Rewards, and Penalties are presented to your kids, you remain free to ignore their claims that they're being shortchanged relative to their siblings. After all, you designed the Goals and consequences to be fair and age-appropriate, not to be equal. Notice that Derek has more Target Goals, and he will receive both greater Rewards and Penalties than his sister or brother.

For Tim and Linda, a general chores item for Annie makes sense and is easy to include. Target Goal #7 becomes: "She will do household and yard chores as requested by her parents." Annie, being too young to realize that chores are not supposed to be fun, loves to help her parents in the house and garden anyway. The additional Goal just formalizes what she has already been doing.

Annie doesn't need a homework Goal because she still finds schoolwork to be an enjoyable pastime. In fairness to her brothers, it must be noted that second grade homework is significantly less demanding than fifth grade or ninth grade homework. Her twin passions are horses (there's a surprise for a seven-year-old girl) and reading. The latter explains why her program doesn't include a reading item. In fact, Linda and Tim joke that Annie might need a Target Goal to *limit* the amount of time she spends with her books, especially the ones about horses!

Finally, it goes without saying (at least by this time) that Target Goal #8 is the Three-Time Rule.

Annie's final Target Goals list look like this:

1. No more tantrums—this includes snorting, stamping, door slamming, and yelling.

2. She will clean her room before leaving for school each morning and before noon on weekends and in the summer. Room cleaning means straightening the bed, picking up all items that don't belong on the floor, and putting dirty laundry in the hamper.

3. She will put away her clean clothes, when they are placed on her bed, by 9:00 P.M. on the day that they are placed there.

4. She will not call her brothers names. When they tell her that they don't want to do something, she will accept it without asking them more than twice. She will not hit, kick, pinch, push, or throw them.

5. Annie will feed the dogs every other day before leaving for school and before noon on weekends and in the summer.

6. She will put away items from one activity before starting another.

7. She will do household and yard chores as requested by her parents.

8. The Three-Time Rule.

Annie gets freebies whenever there are no clean clothes to put away, when Patrick has to feed the dogs, and when there are no special chores requested of her. She also gets credit on days when she doesn't have a tantrum, call her brothers names, leave her stuff around, or violate the Three-Time Rule.

REWARDS AND PENALTIES

The selection of Rewards for this family is fairly simple. After all, the program is being set up as a simple allowance system. On the other hand, keep in mind that there is nothing to stop you from constructing a nontraditional allowance system. If Rewards other than money are more sensible and appropriate for your children, you should certainly feel free to use them. Even when designing a program in which a monetary allowance would likely be chosen as the Reward, I would have asked Linda and Tim to construct the usual list of potential Rewards. It is always possible that something could appear there that would improve the program. Because of our previous experience with choosing Rewards for Bryan's program, however, I will spare you the necessity of repeating this process for Derek, Patrick, and Annie.

Derek likes a lot of things. He likes candy, video games, sports equipment, and television. But what Derek likes most is money. With money, he can buy candy (when his parents allow it), video games, and sports equipment. He can watch television whether he has money or not. When asked directly, and even when not asked at all, Derek has made it clear that he is interested in having money.

Patrick is most interested in having basketball cards, although he is always asking Tim and Linda for the money with which to buy them. He is more than willing to work in exchange for currency. Annie seems to like money, but her family notices that she never spends even a single cent. It can be expected that during their later teen years, on particularly important date nights, the boys will be begging Annie for loans. Depending on the prime rate in effect at that time, she can probably do quite well for herself. In any event, it is decided that the daily Reward will be one-seventh of a weekly cash allowance for each of the children.

This is going to require a little bit of thinking and calculating. Derek has been receiving $5.00 a week for occasionally taking care of his responsibilities, and $10.00 in addition for mowing the lawn. His parents feel that a $15.00 weekly allowance is appropriate for Derek's new list of Target Goals. Of course, 15 can't be divided very neatly by 7. Here comes that old instant raise again. In consideration of Derek's newly expanded household and school obligations and of the fact that he is actually going to take care of them, Tim and Linda settle on a daily Reward of $2.50, or $17.50 per week. Happy kid! Patrick will get a raise from his chore-free $3.00 a week to 75¢ a day, or $5.25 a week. Annie will jump from $2.00 a week to 50¢ a day, or $3.50 a week. More happy kids!

The Bonus and Big Bonus Rewards are also going to be cash in this all-allowance system. Once again, you should feel comfortable in using whatever longer-term Rewards make the most sense for your children. Derek and Patrick are clear about wanting all the loot that they can possibly get their hands on. Annie really wants a horse instead. She is, however, willing to settle for the money with which she could eventually buy a horse. Derek's weekly Bonus Reward is set at $3.50, Patrick's at $1.50, and Annie's at $1.00. Linda and Tim, feeling that a month of perfect performance by their children would be a miracle equivalent to Moses' parting of the Red Sea, select that as the time period in which each child could earn the Big Bonus Reward. They go with $20.00 for Derek, $10.00 for Patrick, and $7.00 for Annie. Expensive? Perhaps, but they decide that it will be well worth it.

The Penalties for these kids are also pretty easy to figure out. They all love to watch television. The all love to play outside. They all fight fiercely every night to stay up as late as they possibly can. If you remember our discussion of consequences in Chapter 4, you will already know that the bedtime Penalty is tailor-made for Derek, Patrick, and Annie. Tim and Linda have already courageously decided that, for their children, fair does not have to be equal. Derek is older, has more responsibilities, and is getting a higher allowance than his siblings. His parents decide that his Penalty will be a twenty-minute subtraction from his normal bedtime for each missed Goal. Patrick and Annie will be given a fifteen-minute deduction for each Penalty. These Penalties will add up in the usual way, including multiple Penalties for repeated misses on a single Goal (such as the one about name-calling).

Tim and Linda are not certain that the Rewards and Penalties they have selected are sufficient to bring about a real improvement in Derek's school performance. They know that the program will help with his homework and basic test preparation, but they are concerned about how much effort Derek will actually put into his studies. Therefore, we decide to bring out the really big guns. After all, this is war!

There is something coming up in Derek's life that overshadows even basketball and video games. No, I'm not talking about girls. He has given his parents all the necessary clues by begging them over and over to take him driving in local parking lots. He is almost fifteen, and he is desperate to drive. Linda and Tim assess his eagerness by mentioning to him that perhaps his driving future will be linked to his school performance. They know they have hit the bull's-eye when he first objects strenuously and then pretends that this possibility doesn't bother him in the least. Score!

Instead of writing a Target Goal about studying, we decide to capitalize on Derek's automotive longings through the use of a novel, off-the-Chart Reward/Penalty. He is told that all future driving, including practicing, licensing, and soloing, depends upon his level of academic achievement. Since a grade of "C" is considered average, and since Tim and Linda are convinced that they have only above-average children, Derek is told that there will be no driving at all unless he maintains an average of "C+" or above (Hallelujah!) in all of his classes. This will be measured at the end of each and every marking period for the rest of his high school career. As long as he achieves this level of performance, his parents will continue to take him out for occasional parking lot driving practice in support of his eventual licensing. After he is licensed, driving privileges will depend on maintaining this grade average.

I think that this is a nice touch, and one that you might consider using in addition to the standard program. It should be saved for genuinely important situations, however, such as inadequate school performance. For this type of Reward/Penalty to be effective, you will need to determine which activity is appropriate to your child's age and deepest desires.

Once the Target Goals, Rewards, and Penalties lists are finished for each child, the program progresses exactly as it did for our friend Bryan. Information is given to the children in the same ways and at the same times as for Bryan. Three different Charts are constructed and, almost every day, three different Rewards are given out. Communication about the program becomes a daily ritual (no doubt) between the mother and father, who lavish praise upon their newly successful children.

Linda and Tim become widely envied as the kids develop into models for the whole community. Because of their parenting accomplishments, they are the talk of the town, advancing in their careers and gaining high political and social position. Unfortunately, the other local children begin to severely resent Derek, Patrick, and Annie after being forced to undergo frequent, unflattering comparisons to these now celebrated siblings. Tim and Linda's children are shunned by their former friends. They are mercilessly taunted by the children whose parents hadn't bothered to read this book. Naturally, those parents are just not able to help their children attain the same measure of academic and social success that have come to Linda and Tim's kids.

Not to worry! As a psychologist, my job is to help. To remedy this unfortunate situation, for which I must shoulder a large portion of the blame, I will most certainly be sending Tim and Linda the first copy of my forthcoming, hypothetical book, _Helping Your Nerdy Child Cope._ It should happen to all of us.

*S*ingle Parents, Divorce, Ex-Partners, and Stepfamilies

A large percentage of the children who find their way to my office spend most of their time living with only one parent. This is not at all surprising, given the current statistics regarding the incidence and prevalence of divorce in our culture. In addition, a variety of nontraditional family structures have sprung up alongside the conventional nuclear and extended families of the "old days." Single women are choosing to become single mothers through sexual intercourse or artificial insemination. Homosexual couples are providing loving homes in which to raise children. Adoption has allowed both men and women to accept the challenges of single parenting. Divorces and births out of wedlock have created an unprecedented number of households in which one parent raises one or more children.

Given the number of forms in which today's families are found, the nomenclature used to label or characterize them can become bewilderingly complex. Unwieldy descriptions, such as "single parents (including both those who have always been single and those who have become single through the death of a spouse or other partner), as well as parents who are divorced and whose ex-spouses are no longer significantly involved with their children (and including the individuals who were never married, but were part of a couple that lived together, and who are now physically separated from the child's other parent)", can make reading feel much like running a marathon, while underwater. In order to avoid this potential literary disaster, for our purposes "divorce" will be taken to mean that a living parent who once resided in the household has left, whether or not the couple was ever legally married. Unless otherwise noted, divorce will also include permanent separation. When it is necessary for clarity, the specific type of divorced or single parent under discussion will be described.

THE TWO GROUPS

Although there are many different types of single parents, each with individual characteristics and specific concerns, a closer look reveals that there are two broad groups into which all of the categories fit. First, there are the parents who are raising their children entirely by themselves, with no "life-partner" (as distinct from roommates, tenants, and friends) living permanently in the same household. Despite the fact that they may be able to have discussions with their friends and family members about raising the children, these parents ultimately bear complete responsibility for the task. Although it is certainly somewhat arbitrary, I will be categorizing these folks as the "single parents." This group includes:

1. Parents who were always single and who had children through sexual intercourse, adoption, or artificial insemination.

2. Parents who were part of a relatively stable, married or unmarried couple, and whose partner died.

3. Parents who were part of a relatively stable, married or unmarried couple, who divorced or separated, and whose ex-partner died.

4. Parents who were part of a relatively stable, married or unmarried couple, who divorced or separated, and whose ex-partner is not currently participating in decision-making regarding the children.

This gets pretty complicated, doesn't it? The last category is made up of parents who have been granted sole custody, or whose ex-partners are completely uninvolved with the children. It also includes those parents whose ex-partner may have significant contact with the children, but who do not have a relationship with the other parent that would allow for meaningful, joint decision-making (see "The Conflicted Divorce" and "The Hostile Ex-Partner" sections below). Under these conditions, any choices that relate to raising the children are made by the more custodial parent. In all of these cases, the single parent has not formed another couple with a new partner. I can't claim that this is an exhaustive list, but I've provided it in order to give you some feeling for the type of parent that I will be referring to as single.

The second group is made up of those biological parents who have divorced, but who are still more or less firmly attached to the other parent. Each ex-partner continues to share in the joys and burdens of child-rearing. At some time in the past, they may have lived together as a couple in the same home. These parents are generally not living in the same household at present, but they are both actively involved in some degree of decision-making about the children. Although the amount of direct contact between the kids and each parent can vary over a wide range, major decisions regarding the children are usually shared by the two adults.

There can also be tremendous variability in how smoothly the joint aspects of parenting are handled by these estranged partners. For example, I have worked with folks who were actually better able to work together on parenting issues once they were physically separated. This is a very desirable outcome in a potentially difficult situation. I also once knew a fellow whose approach to post-divorce parenting involved a drive-by shooting of his ex-wife's mailbox. It's just my opinion, but I think that there were probably more constructive ways that he could have expressed his feelings.

A variety of arrangements, involving both physical custody and decision-making, can be found among this group. Children may spend the same amount of time with each parent, or they may live with one and have "visitations" with the other. Decisions regarding the kids may be equally shared by the parents, or one parent may have the final say as to what is appropriate for the children. The common factor in the group that I am categorizing here as "divorced parents" is that two parents, having had children together through adoption, artificial insemination, or the old-fashioned way, have parted company while continuing to be actively involved in decision-making regarding their kids. This group includes:

1. Parents who were part of a relatively stable, married or unmarried couple, who have divorced or separated, and who have a supportive relationship with the ex-partner.

2. Parents who were part of a relatively stable, married or unmarried couple, who have divorced or separated, and who have a hostile and conflicted relationship with the ex-partner.

3. Parents who were part of a relatively stable, married or unmarried couple, who have divorced or separated and then repartnered (an explanation of, and apology for, this new word will be provided shortly), and who have a supportive relationship with the ex-partner.

4. Parents who were part of a relatively stable, married or unmarried couple, who have divorced or separated and then repartnered, and who have a hostile and conflicted relationship with the ex-partner.

And you thought that the single parents list was complicated?

I will ask you to forgive me for coining the verb "to repartner." You're going to be seeing it quite a few times through the rest of this chapter. To avoid frequent, lengthy, and certainly boring explanations of just who I'm talking about, I needed one word that would cover all of the ways in which new couples get together after previous couples have come apart. Therefore, to repartner is defined here as the act of becoming a couple (relatively stable, married or unmarried, of course) when at least one of the new partners has previously uncoupled. I believe that I'm allowed to make up at least one new word per book.

There are also two additional categories that I will include with the divorced parents, despite the fact that the fit is not an exact one:

5. Parents who have repartnered after the death of a spouse or partner.
6. Previously single parents who later partnered (became part of a couple).

Although there might have been no original partner, or that partner is no longer present, the existence of a new mate provides the logic for placing these folks in this group. Since the additional person also assumes a parental role in the family, we will expand the rule for inclusion in this group to say that decisions regarding the children are shared with another parent, or with a partner who is acting as a parent.

In two of the aforementioned types of divorced parents, the relationship between the custodial and the estranged parent is characterized by significant conflict. For the second category (divorced or separated, who have a hostile and conflicted relationship with the ex-partner), it should be assumed that major decisions regarding the children are still being made jointly despite any continuing friction between the parents. The fourth category (divorced or separated and then repartnered, who have a hostile and conflicted relationship with the ex-partner) includes a new partner who is now acting in a parental role. This type of couple should be included here whether or not the estranged, biological parent is currently involved in decisions about the children. Again, the common thread in this group is that there are two parents, or partners acting as parents, who are actively involved in making choices about what is appropriate for the children. Later on in this chapter, we will be addressing the special difficulties built into improving the behavior of children who are members of stepfamilies.

I want to emphasize that the two groups, single and divorced parents, and the several categories included in each one, are rather arbitrary. They have been constructed in order to facilitate a discussion that can easily get quite bogged down in the details of who belongs where. Although there is very little that is just black or white in divorce, repartnering, and single parenting, it is an exercise in futility to try to list all of the possible grays. For example, if consideration were to be given to the degree of involvement that an ex-partner has with the children, the number of categories could quickly become infinite. I am a simple man. I will simply leave it at these two groups: the single parents, who are raising their children alone, and the divorced parents, who retain some measure of partnership in this undertaking.

SINGLE PARENTS

That having been said, I must now point out that there is a further division in our single parents group. (And this is designed to *minimize* confusion.) The categories that I have listed here include parents who have always been single and parents who have become single after having had their children. Although there is some overlap in the approaches to child-raising of the parents in these two subgroups, there are significant differences between them as well.

Those of you who have always been single are accustomed to having sole responsibility for your children. From the very beginning, you have accepted the role of providing the security, nurturance, love, and guidance that are necessary to your children's healthy development. Although challenges to your parental authority may have developed over time, this in no way changes that fact that you have the exclusive franchise for parenting in your household.

The parents in this first subgroup are naturally empowered by their always-single status to supply any boundaries, limits, or discipline that their children require. When behavioral difficulties arise, they are in a position to decide independently whether a comprehensive program, such as the one that has been described in this book, might be beneficial to the family. There is never a question as to what should be done when one parent disagrees with the other's plan of action. Although questions about consistency might still be valid, those regarding unity are nonexistent. It is only if and when a child challenges their disciplinary authority that these folks might have some doubts regarding their power to parent. But you can relax. This usually happens only when the kids are in their "Terrible" (choose one) Twos/Threes/Fours/Sevens/Adolescence/All of the aboves.

What about those parents who didn't start out as single, but who have ended up that way as the result of one of the circumstances previously described? Here, the concept of empowerment is often the main concern. It is certainly always possible that their children will easily accept the idea that two parents' authority is now exercised by just one. Although this is not an infrequent outcome, it is always a very lucky one. In this situation, parenting continues without the necessity of a pause to develop a new disciplinary style or approach. It is essentially equivalent to always having been a single parent with well-behaved and obedient children.

The problem for parents who have become single is that it is also not unusual for their children to reject them as the sole disciplinarians in the household. This can happen for a variety of reasons. It is not at all unusual, for example, for children to express their anger about the loss of one parent by not accepting direction from the other. They might be less willing to obey a remaining parent of the same sex as themselves. They might not listen to a parent of the opposite sex. I mentioned in Chapter 1 that, in my opinion, it is a child's job to reach for as much freedom and control as possible. The absence of one parent may make this goal appear to be that much more attainable. Finally, in complete fairness to parents who have become single, consideration must also be given to the fact that many of their children were quite sufficiently difficult when there were two parents trying to deal with them.

Newly single parents can often feel completely overwhelmed by the demands of solo child-rearing. The verbal symptoms of this condition, as they are presented in my office, often follow a similar pattern: "They just won't listen to me. I don't know what to do. I can't make them do anything. I try to send them to their rooms, but they refuse to go. What am I supposed to do? Carry them? They're too big, and they won't stay there anyway." I continue to be surprised at the number of times that this type of complaint is stated directly in front of the children. At that moment, you can be sure that the kids are in complete control of the household.

The issue here, again, is one of empowerment. These parents, in attempting to deal with their children's difficult behavior, have become convinced that they do not have the ability to enforce discipline without another person's assistance. I could not disagree with them more. The problem is that there is no outside authority to "deputize" these parents and convince them of their own power. They are forced to learn for themselves that they can handle the situation. Unfortunately, when they let their kids know how powerless they feel about enforcing discipline, these parents are taking a huge step in the wrong direction.

The first requirement for exercising authority with your children is to act as if you have it. You do! You must empower yourself in this way whether or not you truly experience your own parental competence. Unless you appear to be sure of yourself, you will be providing your children with a loophole large enough for them to drive through with an eighteen-wheeler. When single parents fail to convey the idea that they are in control of discipline, it is equivalent to one partner's undermining the other in a couple. The authority is there if you are willing to exert it. You *can* do it. If appearing to be confident in your parenting role requires acting and sales-manship, then your first job is to become an actor and a salesperson. What is then required is a good set of tools and resources to get the disciplinary task done.

The approach to improving children's behavior that I have described in this book is exactly such a tool set. It can be used, with very few modifications, both by parents who have always been single and by those who have become single. Obviously, all of the list construction is carried out by only one person in these situations. This is not to say that advice and support shouldn't be solicited from friends and family members. They can be a tremendous resource in generating ideas and helping you to feel that you are not working in isolation.

It is also not to say that shortcuts should be taken. The steps that were recommended in the previous chapters should be followed in order. Don't be tempted to skip around just because you know what's supposed to come next and there's no one else there to nag and criticize you about not following the directions. You should have little difficulty in finding someone who, if you ask them nicely, would be willing to help nag and criticize (maybe I should start a telephone service for exactly this purpose: "1-800-CALL-NAG"?). If you take shortcuts, you will run the risk of denying yourself sufficient raw material with which to develop a solid and successful program.

Single parents have to double their efforts in providing information and enthusiasm to the kids as the program is developed. In this situation, the hints about Target Goals, Rewards, and Penalties that are dropped by each partner in a couple must all be handled by one individual. There is some compensation for having to do all of this extra work, however. Although designing the system may be somewhat more difficult for a parent who is alone, there is never any danger that a partner will somehow undermine disciplinary authority. Similarly, potential misunderstandings about the mechanics of running the program are divided exactly in half. The daily communication period certainly becomes easier when the "discussion" is entirely in the mind of one individual.

The communication period is an aspect of this approach that requires special attention from single parents. There is a definite tendency for these folks to think, "Communicate? With whom? Why should I set aside a time to think about the program when I think about it all the time anyway? I already know everything about what I'm doing. After all, I'm the only one who's doing it." Wrong. Mistake. Error. It has been my experience that a formal, daily time for "communication" about the program is just as important for single parents as for their coupled counterparts. There is usually no one else in the household to help find and solve the problems that inevitably arise from using this approach. Unless time is specifically set aside for reviewing each day's disciplinary events, small annoyances can quickly grow into major disasters. Nip them in the bud.

The types of questions that single parents should be asking themselves during this daily time for reflection are the same as those discussed in Chapter 6: Which Target Goals were missed? Were the Penalties given immediately? What was the child's reaction? Was the Three-Time Rule used appropriately? Is there anything in the program that's confusing to anyone? Are there loopholes that need to be closed? Are the Target Goals, Rewards, and Penalties working well, or are changes needed? Is there more fine-tuning to be done? Did any Time-Outs go well?

Most importantly, just as it is for couples, this is the best time to examine any repeating behavior problems that you didn't include in your original Target Goals. You will then be able to prepare yourself for the next time that they appear by adding them to the Chart. It is also a good time to determine whether those Goals that have outlived their usefulness need to be adjusted or dropped.

Parents, whether single, divorced, or partners in an intact couple, can become overwhelmed by having to deal with very difficult children. Single parents do not have the option of sharing their child-raising problems, and the attempts to find solutions for them, with a live-in ally. They often feel that there are fewer resources available to them in meaningfully addressing their children's negative behaviors.

The behavioral program described in this book is one approach that can be of tremendous help when things seem to be totally out of control. If you have tried this method, but you are still having major problems with your children, don't disempower yourself by telling your kids that you are giving up. Instead, please take a look at Chapter 11, "Troubleshooting". Further adjustments that can be made to the program are described there. Information about getting outside help and support is also provided. Finally, there is material about what might be done when all else, including this program (gasp), has failed. I've said that if what you're doing isn't working after you have given it a fair trial, then you should stop doing it and try something else. Even though it may break my heart to say so, this advice also applies to the method of helping children behave that I have presented here.

DIVORCED PARENTS

You will recall that, by my definition, divorced parents share the child-raising decisions with an ex-partner, a new partner, or both. As you might expect by now, I have also managed to divide the divorced parents into two subgroups. The first is made up of those parents whose ex-partner is generally positive and supportive in sharing decisions about raising the children. The second is characterized by the continuation of significant conflict between the two original parents. Whether because of issues related to their relationship, or because of differences in opinion about what is the correct way to bring up the kids, these folks have not been able to work together without an excessive amount of arguing. It is not at all surprising that the first group provides less difficulty for your average psychologist.

If you fall into the subgroup whose supportive ex-partners share the major decisions regarding child-rearing, you should consider yourself to be truly blessed. When estranged parents are able to put aside their differences in favor of supporting their children's best interests, the potential benefits to those children cannot be overstated. Through the years, I have seen a great deal of research material regarding the effects that divorce and separation have on kids. The conclusions are generally so dismal that it is a wonder to me that any child in this situation can avoid a guaranteed future as a substance abuser or a serial murderer!

The fact is, however, that all of us know many children who are the products of broken families and who seem to be in pretty good shape. With more and more marriages ending in divorce, it is critically important to determine the factors that are involved in allowing children to survive this event and then go on to flourish. What is the secret ingredient, hidden from researchers, that can make this happen?

I believe that the single most important element in raising well-adjusted, post-divorce children is the attitude of their biological parents. If these parents can: 1) avoid either serious arguments or sniping at each other in front of the children, 2) keep themselves from saying negative things to the kids about the other parent, 3) prevent themselves from "pumping" their children for information regarding the ex-partner, 4) refrain from using their offspring to exchange negative messages, child support checks, or alimony payments with the other parent, and 5) keep young ears from overhearing nasty telephone conversations, then there is an excellent chance for the kids to get through the divorce in fine style. In order to protect children from some of the major problems that can be part of the divorce process, the necessity of acting in ways that serve the best interests of those children should *always* be uppermost in everyone's mind. You can be sure that I will have much more to say about all of this later in the chapter.

When you have a supportive ex-partner, whether or not you have repartnered, you are in a good position to help improve your children's difficult behavior. If you are the primary, custodial parent, for example, you can design and run the behavioral program in your household with the expectation that your ex-partner will enthusiastically support your efforts. The other parent's assistance can include such things as expressing interest about the program directly to the children, encouraging them to do their best, demonstrating pride in their improving behavior, giving you moral support in your undertaking, or even helping with the construction of the program.

If you have not repartnered, you have the option of either doing the design work by yourself or including your ex-partner. A repartnered couple can also choose whether or not to solicit the participation of a non-custodial parent for this project. In any event, it is important that this supportive ex-partner be aware of exactly what you are doing about discipline and how it is going. At the very least, the kids will certainly be discussing the system during their visits to the non-custodial household. Enough information should be exchanged so that the other parent can participate meaningfully in these conversations. A supportive ex-partner should be considered an invaluable ally in any attempt to help your children behave.

If the non-custodial parent is having similar behavioral problems with the children, he or she can choose to run the same program, or a similar version, in the visited household. Even if the difficult behaviors don't appear in the other home, due to such factors as the children's being there for less time, there are benefits to having the same program running in each residence. A consistent approach to discipline between the two households can only serve to reinforce parental expectations and accelerate the children's behavioral improvement.

When two amicable, divorced, unrepartnered ("unrepartnered"? Sorry!) parents will be using the same program in separate households, it is recommended that they consider the possibility of doing the design and construction work together. Two heads may not always be better than one, but in the case of helping difficult children behave, a willing ex-partner can be a worthy resource. This work should be done in exactly the same fashion as described for intact couples, but probably without the addition of candlelight and wine. Even an occasional, formal communication period (either in person or by telephone) can be a valuable element in a separated couple's program.

The situation is not too much more complicated for custodial parents who have a supportive ex-partner as well as a new partner. Here, the construction of the program must always include the primary, custodial couple. If the system is going to be running in two households, and if this couple is willing to include the ex-partner in the design process, so much the better. Three heads might be better than two. *Definitely* no candlelight and wine, however. In those cases where the ex-partner is unavailable for one reason or another, the program is constructed by the new couple in the usual way.

The situation is considerably more complicated when you have repartnered and your ex-partner is hostile to you, to your current partner, to your attempts at improving your children's behavior, or to some combination of these (see "The Conflicted Divorce" and "The Hostile Ex-Partner" sections below). All is not lost, however, since you now have that new and supportive companion with whom to do the necessary work. If both your new partner *and* your ex-partner refuse to join you in trying to improve the kids' difficult behavior, I can only recommend that you undertake a long and expensive course of individual psychotherapy in order to help you determine how you got into this mess!

The Conflicted Divorce

I believe that more damage has been done to children's mental health by the post-divorce conflict between their parents than by any other single cause (with the possible exception of alcohol abuse or dependency in the family). While it is true that the kids who have successfully navigated through this most difficult situation would be unlikely to appear in my office, it is also true that a great number of the children I see have received psychological bruises from their battling, divorced parents.

In almost all of these cases, each parent feels completely justified in holding fast to his or her position, no matter how much conflict is going on or how much negative effect it's having on the kids. Both parents are usually quite certain that it is the other one who is causing all of the trouble. Although there are definitely situations in which one of the divorced parents is primarily responsible for the problems that are emotionally injuring their children, the more frequent scenario involves two, well-meaning adults who cannot stop warring even when they know that innocent bystanders are becoming victims.

The difficulty here for psychologists and other mental health professionals is in getting the estranged parties to cooperate for the sake of their children. To say that this can be a troublesome undertaking is a vast understatement. The most popular reason for the couple to have separated in the first place is that they just couldn't get along. A therapist or counselor who simply states the fact that the parents should work together because it would be good for the children should be prepared to play the lead role in the road production of *Pollyanna in Hell.* Everyone knows that a conflicted, post-divorce relationship between the parents is bad for the kids. Doing something about it, however, proves to be the hard part.

Even with that having been said, when I am working with divorced parents in my office, I always start by explaining the obvious. If a child's parents have separated, and if that child is having behavioral difficulties, I will eventually do my best to get these parents to come in together. This attempt will be made even if one or both of them have repartnered. Even if they hate each other. I've worked with separated parents who have been able to stop or, at least, change their pattern of quarreling after one basic discussion of the harm that they could be causing to their children.

I've also worked with parents who can't, or won't, stop their course of destruction no matter what is said to them, how it is said, how many times it is said, or by whom it is said. They appear to be blind to the fact that their behavior is going to leave emotional scars on their children, and that the scars can be permanent. Sometimes, these folks choose to ignore even their own kids' reports of the psychological damage that is being done.

Please don't think that I am being overly dramatic by using words and phrases such as "psychological bruises," "damage," "emotionally injuring," "victims," "harm," "destruction," and "emotional scars." My office is the perfect vantage point from which to see the results of serious, post-divorce conflict. Some of these effects can be seen immediately in the children's moods and behaviors. Others can be present throughout the entire course of a lifetime. For this reason, I'm going to use a few gallons of ink to convince those of you who are exposing your children to this type of conflict that you should make some significant changes. I will also make some suggestions about what those changes should be and how to implement them. This is truly an excellent example of a situation in which an ounce of prevention is *far* better than a pound of cure. The behavioral program that I have described in this book can be quite effective even when there is antagonism between estranged parents. It will always work better, however, when such friction is minimized.

In the previous section, I made several recommendations about things that should not be happening in your relationship to an ex-partner. I mentioned potential problems with arguing; being negative about the other parent; having information, messages, or payments flowing through the children; and eavesdropping. Let's take a closer look at what can happen to children when their divorced parents don't take care of this business, and at how to minimize such problems.

I believe that one of the worst things a divorced couple can do in front of their children, and one of the things that is done most often, is to have serious arguments. I also believe that ex-partners have every right in the world, constitutionally protected in the United States, to lash out verbally at each other as viciously and frequently as they may wish.

But *not* in front of the kids. It is part of the remarkable nature of most children that, even if they have seen their mother or father behave quite inappropriately, they will almost always do their best to continue loving both of them. This is either their gift or their bane, depending on the subsequent behavior of those parents.

When you and your ex-partner decide to go at it in front of the kids, you are immediately putting them in the position of experiencing a (usually unconscious) demand to make a choice between the two of you. They understand the idea of taking sides in a quarrel. Despite the fact that children often verbally express a preference for one or the other parent, they want to love, and to be loved by, both. The feeling that they are required to make a choice between their estranged parents is highly painful and confusing to most kids. It upsets the balance that they strive for in dealing with a situation that is problematic, at best, by its very nature. If you doubt that this is true, take a look at the child whose estranged, embattled parents both show up unexpectedly at a soccer game. In that type of situation, the child's attempts to navigate through such choices as where to stand and how to act can result in an emotional meltdown.

Why should this lead to difficult behavior on the part of the kids? As grown-ups, we have developed a variety of ways to deal with our negative emotions. We can seethe, deny, rant and rave, discuss calmly (always a good idea at some point), use the energy to do something positive, break something, get depressed, and so forth. Children, being at an earlier stage of psychological development, have a much smaller palette of emotional expression from which to choose. As discussed in Chapters 4 and 7, they are not yet adept at using abstraction as a tool for dealing with their environment. This is frequently what prevents them from understanding both sides of an argument, or the very fact that an argument might actually have two understandable sides.

Ṣtrong, negative emotions can quickly become overwhelming to them. If these feelings are not verbalized or expressed directly (through crying or shouting, for example), they often manifest themselves through a child's oppositional, defiant, or uncontrollable behaviors.

I want to emphasize the fact that I am not saying that you and your ex-partner shouldn't argue. Not only do I think that this is acceptable, but I believe that you and your *current* partner should also occasionally be airing your differences. I am always more concerned by the couples who come into my office saying that they never clash than by those who acknowledge that they exchange cross words now and then. It is somewhat beyond my understanding that two different people can live together for any length of time in absolutely perfect harmony (although I'm sure it has been known to happen).

When I am told that "never is heard a discouraging word," I usually end up wondering who is hiding or repressing what, and why. This bit of suspiciousness might be considered to be an occupational hazard for those who are in my line of work. As a psychologist, of course, I generally encourage people to try to work out their differences. You might have *every* right to argue with your ex-partner, but, as in any relationship, it's always better if the major issues can actually be resolved. Fix things if you can. If you can't, any leftover quarreling should *not* take place in front of the kids.

The confusion and pressure that children experience when they feel forced to choose between estranged parents is also the reason for you to avoid making negative comments to the kids about your ex-partner. A child may seem to support you in these opinions. It is also possible that the child may become oppositional and defiant toward you in defense of the other parent. You might consider that this child, when in the other household, could also seem to support your ex-partner's negative opinions toward you. Similarly, the child might be oppositional and defiant toward that parent in defense of you. Each of these possible scenarios, in my opinion, represents a true disaster. The child is being put in an impossible situation. Once again, it is a child's job to love both parents. It is your job to support your kids in their need to have a positive relationship with their other parent.

The only exception to this supportive position comes when your ex-partner is a genuine monster toward the children. I am not talking about someone who is simply "Not the Best Parent in the Whole Wide World." I mean an ex-partner whose behavior and attitudes are demonstrably damaging to a child's healthy, psychological or physical development. In these circumstances, although it is certainly not helpful to devalue the other parent directly to the children, it is also not necessary for you to support a positive relationship with that parent. While some explanation of your ex-partner's negative behavior might be necessary to help your children understand the situation, editorializing about that parent's evil motivations should surely be avoided. This can be a very complicated situation, and consultation with a therapist or counselor might be helpful in untangling it. A formal custody evaluation (or reevaluation), done by an independent expert or agency, can also be helpful in these circumstances.

When listening to one member of an estranged couple, it can often be quite difficult to determine whether the other is actually doing something that is harmful to the children, or whether the statements being made have more to do with a continuing, personal conflict. It is frequently impossible for divorced parents to be objective about each other's parenting skills.

If you have not been supporting your ex-partner's relationship with your children, it is quite important that you make an honest appraisal of why this has been happening. Are you truly protecting the best interests of your children, or are your actions more closely related to an ongoing struggle between you and the other parent? In the event that the latter is the case, you should consider doing the difficult work of changing your position to one of support for that parent's relationship with the kids. Again, this is not to say that you should necessarily like your ex-partner. Tolerance may be all that is needed. Such a change in your attitude is required solely to create the most positive environment for your children's development.

If you feel that you need some help in getting your ex-partner to understand your concerns about how the kids are being treated; if your ex-partner completely, frequently, and loudly disagrees with you about what is best for the children; if you are not entirely sure that your negative opinion about your ex-partner's parenting is accurate; or if the other people you value have stopped supporting your position; then I would strongly recommend that you consider having the entire situation evaluated by an outside expert. The way to find the right person for this job is discussed in Chapter 11.

I also frequently suggest that parents who have decided to divorce, or who have already separated, think about the possibility of getting into couples therapy. How's *that* for a strange sense of timing? The explanation is that this recommendation is not intended as a last-ditch attempt to repair their damaged relationship. (I always encourage parents to actively explore *every* possible remedy before reaching the decision to divorce.) Rather, it is based entirely on my feeling that divorcing parents should work hard to resolve any conflicts that might have a continuing, negative impact on their children.

Let's examine the next behavior through which estranged grown-ups can cause problems for their kids. Eavesdropping by children whose parents have separated is one of my favorite topics. Actually, eavesdropping by *any* children is one of my favorite topics. It never ceases to amaze me how little parents know about the advanced, intelligence-gathering skills of their own offspring. CIA? FBI? NSC? These operations are small potatoes compared to the spying ability of your average, household-variety child.

I have learned to love those office sessions during which a divorced parent tells me that, despite the fact that there is a tremendous amount of conflict with an ex-partner, the children know nothing about it. I always try very hard not to laugh. This earnest pronouncement almost always follows the previous week's session with the child, during which I got to view both sides of the post-marital discord in detail that is usually available only from satellite reconnaissance photographs. I recall something about little pitchers having big ears. While I don't have a clue about what that actually means, I do know that kids hear *everything*.

In the situation I am describing, there is no active attempt by a grown-up to influence the attitudes or behavior of a child. Instead, the child may make decisions about how to act toward each parent based solely on information that has been accidentally, or intentionally, overheard. The result here can be very much the same as when parents argue in front of their children or make negative statements to the kids regarding the ex-partner. These children can feel forced to choose, or pretend to choose, between their parents. They are very likely to express their confused emotions through difficult behavior. Your next job is to cut off the underground flow of information that can lead to this unfortunate circumstance.

What is the children's best source of unofficial, unauthorized, and uncontrolled data about their parents' past and present relationship? You guessed it, the telephone. Even parents who carefully avoid discussing divorce issues in person when the kids are around will often forget that one side of a telephone conversation can easily be overheard by anyone in the general vicinity. It can be picked up by kids who are just hanging around the area, and it can certainly be heard by kids who are particularly interested in finding out everything they can about the subject. This is true whether you have telephoned a close friend to pleasantly discuss your ex-partner's multiple shortcomings, or whether your side of a phone call with the other parent is rattling windows all over the neighborhood. In other words, don't say negative things about your ex-partner to anyone, in person or over the telephone, unless you are *absolutely certain* that your kids are asleep (*really* asleep), out of state, at forestry school, or in the soundless vacuum of interstellar space.

If you truly want to put your children directly in the middle of the conflict between you and your ex-partner, I would highly recommend using them to carry negative messages, child support payments, or alimony checks back and forth between the two households. Alternately, you might consider pumping them for information about the other parent's personal life each time that they return from a visit. Either of these approaches should result in a complete disaster for the kids.

In the first case, whether or not this is your intention, you will magnify a child's perception that a choice between parents is being requested or required. When children are actually used as emissaries for bad tidings ("Tell your father/mother that I think he/she is a complete idiot"), no imagination at all is required for them to draw the conclusion that they have been drafted into one of two opposing armies. As I mentioned previously, this is destructive to children even when they appear to agree with your position in the conflict.

Unless the other parent is a saint (a proposition with which, at this point, you would most likely disagree), negative messages from you that are delivered through the kids are going to be met with extremely negative reactions. Your kids will be having enough trouble dealing with the divorce without having to bear the brunt of emotional responses that, rightfully, should be directed at you. If there is bitter medicine to be taken in this regard, take it yourself. You are there to protect your children, not the other way around. Of course, if there is arguing to be done with the other parent, I have no doubt that you'll be doing it when the kids aren't in the area. Right?

The situation is very much the same when you use your children to deliver or request those hotly contested child support and alimony payments. Here's a topic that doesn't have *too* much emotional baggage attached to it. In my office, I have only one thing to say about conflicts around these payments, and it seldom satisfies anyone but me. Nevertheless, I believe the advice to be good, and I will pass it on to you. If you and your ex-partner have really tried, but you can't work out your financial arrangements together, call your lawyer.

Now, now. Don't be that way. I know that you may be hoping to avoid more legal entanglements and expenses. I know that you might not have had much luck with working through the legal system in the past. I also know that child support and alimony can be highly technical and emotional issues that can require the advice of an attorney. I never ask lawyers to provide psychotherapy and, in return, I try to avoid giving legal advice. If you need help in resolving the financial aspects of your divorce settlement, call a lawyer. If you want to explore your *feelings* about these conflicts, then by all means, call a psychologist.

Issues around child support and alimony can be extremely difficult for the two involved adults. They should *never* cause emotional upset for your children. This is another case in which your job is to protect the kids from some of the nasty realities of grown-up life. The chances are huge that unpleasant comments will be made to the "delivery-child" by either the paying or the receiving parent. Even if nothing is actually said, a child can easily become aware of the negative emotional climate that often exists around these exchanges.

The circumstances are even worse when a child is required to ask for missing payments, or to report back about the reasons that they are not forthcoming. Kids do not need to share in the very adult resentments that can be generated here. I would be hard pressed to come up with another way that parents could more completely involve their children in a post-separation conflict. Once again, putting children in this type of situation causes them to feel pressure and confusion about choosing one parent over the other. I advise all parents, including those who do not have unresolved issues in this area, to handle directly any of the verbal and physical transactions that are related to child support and alimony payments. Keep the kids out of it.

Finally, I mentioned that pumping children for personal information about the other parent is not good for their mental health. It is bad enough that kids often become highly skilled at collecting such information on their own. To intentionally turn them into spies just compounds the problem. In this case, the usual issues that are raised when a child feels forced to pledge allegiance to only one parent are present again. Further, there is little that could more totally poison a child's relationship with a parent than having to act as a "mole" in the household.

It is always interesting to me that the parent who has commissioned the child's espionage work generally assumes that the same thing is not going on in the other direction. Quite frequently, it is. Counterintelligence is an occupational hazard in the spy business. When children learn that this type of behavior is both acceptable and valued, there is nothing to keep them from using it to try to get attention and approval from *both* estranged parents. This poison can be spread quite evenly and thickly.

I highly recommend that if you have a question about what's going on in your ex-partner's household, you ask that individual directly. The information that you get from your children in this regard should be limited to what they did while visiting and how much they enjoyed it. Feel free to ask about whether homework was done and what the soccer scores were. If the kids choose to say more, you are certainly free to listen. You are also free to tell them that you are not interested in hearing the minute details of your ex-partner's personal life, and I encourage you to do this. When your children mention some intriguing tidbit, you should carefully consider whether a follow-up question to them is appropriate. If you really want to know more about events in the other household, screw up your courage and go straight to the source. Once again, the best course is to leave the kids out of it.

None of this is to imply that you should ignore your kids when they say things about real problems in your ex-partner's performance as a parent. Follow-up questions here can be quite important. The approach to this type of material should always be gentle and emotionally neutral. When you have enough information to determine that there is truly a problem or an issue, the questioning should immediately shift from the children to the other parent. Did I mention that this should always be done when the kids are elsewhere?

So, we have spent a good deal of time examining the problems that can develop for children whose divorced and embattled parents aren't careful. What does this have to do with the program that I have recommended to help your difficult child behave? Many pages ago, I mentioned that estranged parents who put aside their differences are in an excellent position to help with behavior improvement. I hope that whatever leverage I have gained through describing the often dismal consequences of post-divorce conflict can be put to good use in convincing you to work toward declaring a truce.

Once again, you are free to disagree with each other, to be angry, and to quarrel. You now know how strongly I feel about the necessity of your not sharing any of this with your kids. Here's one more thing about which I've developed some strong feelings. I have become completely convinced that anything you can do to reduce the amount of divorce-related conflict will be of tremendous benefit to your children.

I've used a great many words to discuss the conflicted divorce because it is a subject that's truly dear to my heart. The closer you can come to having the other parent really support you in your disciplinary work, the easier it will be to design and run a solid and effective behavioral program. You will then be in a position where your ex-partner can offer encouragement, help in the construction of the program, or use the same type of program in the other household.

As I stated in the previous section, and as should now be even more clear, those of you who get this kind of support from an estranged partner can consider yourselves to be genuinely lucky. Although I am keenly aware of the paradoxical nature of asking people who were not able to get along with each other during the course of a committed relationship to try to do so after it is over, I urge you to do your best at this in support of your children. Hey, it might be much easier now that you don't also have to deal with your ex-partner's repeatedly squeezing the toothpaste tube from the bottom, refusing to replace the empty toilet paper roll (or putting it on backwards), and making those horribly disgusting little sounds while eating.

The Hostile Ex-Partner

I claimed once before that I do live in the real world. As a psychologist who works with individuals, couples, and families, I am definitely aware that some estranged parents are not going to be able to take the well-intentioned advice that I just offered. Sometimes, the continuing conflict between ex-partners is completely justified, and sometimes it can't be stopped whether it's appropriate or not. This situation certainly adds to the problems in helping your difficult child behave. The question then becomes whether it is possible to improve children's behavior if one parent is indifferent or, worse, hostile to the other parent's approach. When this is the case, bringing about positive change for the children is definitely going to be harder. It is, however, by no means impossible. Consider it to be merely a greater challenge.

If your ex-partner is simply disinterested in your attempts to help your children behave, you are not really in an unworkable situation at all. Whether or not you have repartnered, you can run the program in your household just as it has previously been described here. Although you can feel free to keep the other parent posted as to your progress, this is certainly not a necessity. You alone, or you and your current partner, can completely handle the construction and operation of the system without reference to the other parent's opinions. As I mentioned before, support from the other household is always a welcome addition to the program, but it is never a requirement. At least your ex-partner's detachment will not directly interfere with how you choose to handle discipline in your home.

When two estranged parents are running the behavioral program in their separate households, the resulting consistency provides a great deal of disciplinary reinforcement to the children. If the program is implemented in only one of the households, positive results can still be expected despite the fact that total consistency is not maintained. More to the point, the parent who is following the program will reap all the benefits.

The other parent will likely continue to have the same old problems with getting the kids to behave and take care of their responsibilities. This fact may be of some interest to the grown-ups who have chosen to use this behavioral system, but it is certainly not their problem. I have always felt that, even when an iceberg has been struck, it is not always necessary for everyone to go down with the ship. If you have decided to help your children by using the behavioral approach that I have described, your ex-partner is free to sink, by ignoring your positive efforts, or to swim, by joining you in them.

Since physical custody of the children is not always shared equally by estranged partners, a question is frequently raised regarding what can be done by the "less custodial" parent to improve the kids' behavior. The advice I give in this case is very much the same as the advice I give to "more custodial" parents, to single parents, and to parents who remain in intact couples. Run the program, run the program, and run the program! You may have the children for only a small fraction of the time that your ex-partner has them, but you are certainly allowed to set the rules in your own household.

Make the Target Goals reflect your expectations for the children's behavior when they are with you. Even if you are not in a position to significantly influence the way your kids act during the times that you are not together, this is no reason for you not to improve their behavior when they are in your home. The clear and consistent approach to discipline that you establish will be beneficial to your children even if it's major function becomes that of serving as a good model for *their* future child-raising efforts. As you will see when we get to the "Disneyland Parent" later in this chapter, the program will affect your kids positively even in those cases where they make it painfully clear to you that they much prefer the lax discipline provided by their other parent.

When your ex-partner has gone beyond indifference and is openly hostile to your attempts to discipline the children, you unquestionably have a problem, but by no means an insoluble one. In the worst case, the other parent expresses negative opinions about the program both to you and directly to the kids. If it is only you that is getting the brunt of this bad attitude, you can choose just to ignore it and forge ahead with the job of improving your children's behavior. The situation is somewhat more complicated if the kids are also hearing from your ex-partner that you are going about things in the wrong way. Once again, you might just overlook this obstacle and go about your disciplinary business. There are several other options, however, that you might also consider.

First, most obvious, and frequently most unappealing, is to have a face-to-face (or, at least, mouth-to-telephone) discussion with your ex-partner about the negative attitude and how it is causing difficulties in your household. Given the situation that is to be discussed, it would not be unrealistic for you to expect an unfriendly response to this initiative. In order to help you navigate through these hostile waters, I am prepared to arm you with hundreds of dollars' worth of psychological experience (and at no extra charge) in the next few paragraphs.

The most important thing for you to remember in these delicate negotiations is to talk only about yourself. Although this sounds impossible, your best bet is always to avoid directly discussing either your ex-partner's substantial faults or the negative effects they are having on you and your children. What is to be prevented, when at all possible, is a defensive reaction from the other parent. If you start with accusations, you will most certainly end up with the same old arguments that likely led to your divorce in the first place. This would be a complete waste of everyone's time. Instead, this is a very good time to talk about yourself.

Your sentences should start with "I" or "me" rather than with "you." It is important that you not refer to your ex-partner with phrases such as "always been a complete jerk," "would be just as happy if the kids turned out to be bums," or "parents taught you how to behave, you'd be able to teach the kids." After beginning with "I," focus on your *feelings*. If you present only what you believe to be the facts, you are providing all the raw material that is necessary for a good argument. When I hear you say, "You are purposely trying to make me look bad in front of the children," I hear your ex-partner respond, "I am not, you (fill in the blank with the expletive that you know, from your years of experience, will surely follow)." In this exchange, you have started with what may be a fact, but it is certainly also an accusation. With an aggressive start to the exchange, a defensive reaction can almost always be expected.

Instead, you should begin with your *feelings* about how your ex-partner's attitude is affecting the household. "It makes me feel sad (or hurt, angry, isolated, confused, etc.) when you won't support the rules that I'm trying to get the kids to follow in my home." Then, stop talking. The ball is immediately in the other parent's court, and you should wait to see what happens. There is no room here for a response of, "No, it doesn't." People can argue with what you think and with what you do, but they can never tell you that you don't feel the way that you feel. Yes, there is a mild accusation in the body of the sentence, but it is limited to events that are taking place in your home. This is usually much less threatening to the other parent than such sweeping charges as, "You are totally destroying these children!" After your ex-partner responds, you can certainly expand the conversation beyond your opening sentence, but I advise returning to your feelings if things get too heated. It is often surprising what a difference there can be in your interactions when you start with "I," stick to your feelings, avoid major accusations, and focus on the events in your household.

You may object to this approach as unnecessarily coddling your ex-partner, or as pussyfooting around the issues. It is most important for you to remember what your goal is here. You are not trying to save an already damaged relationship, and you are not trying to iron out all of your differences. Rather, you are trying to create an environment that serves the best interests of your children. Although you don't need the other parent's active participation to make the program successful, your work with the children will certainly be easier if you are supported or, at least, benignly ignored by your ex-partner.

Any problems that are caused when the other parent criticizes the program in front of the kids can also be discussed in this fashion. The point should be made that you are open to considering any and all objections, but that these should be brought directly to you rather than channeled through the children. You can emphasize that this suggestion is based only on your desire to avoid confusing the kids about how they are to behave in *either* household. It might also be important for you to make clear that you are not trying to interfere with the discipline in your ex-partner's home.

If all of this fails to do the job (and, in the real world, it sometimes does), you are left to give up the idea of changing your ex-partner's behavior in favor of discussing the situation with your children. As always, you should not say anything negative to the children about the other parent's hostility toward supporting the behavioral program. This would be equivalent to using your car's high beams to blind an oncoming driver who has refused to lower his. It is definitely better if at least *one* of you can see, and that one might as well be you.

Explain to the kids that each parent has different rules for behavior in the two households, and that you are not concerned by the other parent's criticism of your approach. Let the children know that you will not be influenced by your ex-partner's opinions in this regard, so that they will not try to use this as leverage in getting you to give up on enforcing discipline. When discussing the behavioral program with the kids, emphasize the Rewards and the other positive benefits (such as no more nagging) that they can expect. Do not tell them that the other parent should be doing things the same way that you are. Do tell them that you love them very much.

Keep in mind that your consistent approach to discipline will benefit them for the rest of their lives, no matter how much they might try to convince you otherwise. We will take a look at why this is so when we discuss the "Disneyland Parent."

STEPFAMILIES

Stepparenting. Talk about your double-edged swords. In my office, I frequently hear about the side of this blade that can leave deep wounds when it is wielded clumsily, even when intentions are at their best. I also see how it can be used to help cut through what had previously been the most tangled of knots. Those of you who are stepparents, and those of you who have married them, know that blended families can be the breeding ground for tremendous conflict, tremendous satisfaction, or both.

For purposes of clarity, we will consider stepfamilies (or blended families) to be those in which a divorced parent, with some degree of child custody or visitation rights, has formed another, relatively stable couple with a new partner. Additional children may or may not have been brought into the family by the newcomer, who therefore might have a great deal of experience with kids, or who might have none at all. In any case, I heartily salute those of you who are: 1) helping to raise someone else's children, 2) helping to raise someone else's children as well as your own, 3) letting someone else help you raise your children, or 4) hatching eggs, even though you are an elephant, while Mayzie, that lazy bird, has flown off to Palm Beach for a vacation. No, no, no! Wait a minute. That last one is from a Dr. Seuss book. But I do commend those of you who are the unsung heroes in this often difficult undertaking.

Let me start by saying that the behavioral program I have described here can be extremely helpful for straightening out the confusion in discipline that sometimes follows divorce and repartnering. Getting the kids to behave can be hard enough without the distractions of new people in the house, new authority figures for the kids, and a new blending of disciplinary styles by the grown-ups. If it is true that children will grab for all the freedom that they can get (and I have gone on-record as believing this to be the case), then the multiple changes in parenting that come along with this situation will surely provide them with ample opportunities to make their moves. Even the smoothest transition into a blended family will require some time for everyone to get used to all of the newly adjusted roles and expectations.

When I discussed single parents, I mentioned that children might misbehave as a way of expressing anger about one parent's having left the household. Depending on the attitudes of particular children, there can be a tendency for them to disobey a remaining parent of the same, or of the opposite, sex as themselves. In stepfamilies, the kids may also have to contend with such problems as feeling that they are no longer "The Man/Woman of the House," a position that they may have held for quite some time. They just might not accept the disciplinary authority of any "outsider."

Although I certainly don't believe that a new family member should walk right into a household and expect to change everything, I also don't believe that a repartnered couple should wait too long before developing a comfortable, consistent, and unified style of discipline. A speedy approach to this undertaking is a definite requirement if the kids have had ongoing behavioral difficulties, or if the new relationships in the family are starting to cause them trouble. If things are completely calm for you, then you don't need to be reading this book. You should be writing one instead. Otherwise, the behavioral program can be useful to you in several ways.

First, the very act of constructing this system causes partners to express their specific expectations regarding the kids' behavior. To say the very least, this process can be highly educational for both. If these things aren't said right out loud, there's always the possibility that each parent will be working toward different goals. Would you believe that arguments about discipline could develop? Avoiding this situation is as easy as talking together about what is to be required of the children. An excellent way to organize such a discussion is to develop formal Target Goals, just as I described in Chapters 2 and 3. These Target Goals will provide both a framework for your conversation and a tool to be used in your ongoing behavioral work.

Second, even when new partners agree on the expectations for their children's behavior, they may be worlds apart in their feelings about how to achieve these objectives. Stylistic differences between parents are extremely common when it comes to discipline. Even brand-new parents generally have some pretty definite ideas about how household rules should be enforced. When one or both partners are also bringing several years of child-raising experience into a new couple, these opinions might be completely set in stone.

In Chapter 1, I stated that any style of discipline can be effective if both parents are unified and consistent in applying it. I also said that, in my opinion, the best styles are those that are negotiated compromises between the parents' original positions. When this is the case, the final product gives some expression to what each partner thinks is truly important. The inflexibility that could be a stumbling block for veteran parents can be overcome through the process of working together to design a comprehensive behavioral program.

The next reason for repartnered couples to use the behavioral system is to quickly clarify the new authority structure in the household. I'm sure you'll recognize these old favorites from my greatest hits file: "*You* have no right to tell *me* what to do! *You're* not my father/mother!" "We always did it like this before *you* got here." "My *real* mom/dad told me not to listen to you." And who could ever forget my personal favorite, "You're a *jerk!*"? This kind of stuff can go on for years. This kind of stuff should also be prevented.

The behavioral program can easily be used to show children that both the parent and the stepparent are now equal partners in discipline. This is because it helps the couple in rapidly developing the consistency and unity that I keep insisting are required to improve children's behavior. It should not surprise you by now that I believe this to be the most important reason for new partners to use the system. Children with divorced parents have already gone through at least one major upheaval in the chain of command. It is most likely that there was some level of disruption in discipline related to the original separation. Whether or not the children then accepted the new situation, the addition of yet another authority figure to their lives often leads to great confusion and to the possibility of their displaying some significantly negative behavior.

I've mentioned that a goal and a result of this behavioral program is to make parents completely interchangeable to their children in terms of discipline. This is the factor that makes the program useful for establishing the new lines of authority in a stepfamily. Through implementing this system, the partners become unified in consistently presenting their children with the same consequences for the same behaviors. The Rewards and Penalties are all specified in advance, and they are directly related to clearly defined Target Goals. The children then have no room to maneuver in accusing either parent of favoritism or scapegoating.

Each parent supports the other in this undertaking, closing any loopholes that might allow the kids to consider one parent as the greater, and one as the lesser, disciplinary authority. The stability that this approach provides can be highly beneficial when a family is newly blended or when challenges to the authority of one or both parents develop later.

Another reason that recently repartnered couples should consider using the behavioral program is that it can save them a tremendous amount of time. If they do not have a consistent and unified approach to discipline, months and years can go by as they try to get used to each other's styles and as their children's behavior continues to deteriorate. In many (but not all) stepfamilies, there is often a "honeymoon" period for discipline as the families are initially blended. During this period, there is pure magic in the air. It appears that everyone is going to be great friends, and the kids willingly, even eagerly, accept all of the new couple's suggestions and corrections. Well, perhaps I'm overstating things a bit, but the situation can seem too good to be true. It usually is. Harsh reality often sets in with the first major clash between child and not-biologically-related adult.

The deterioration in children's behavior that can follow a disciplinary honeymoon, and the parents' various attempts to deal with it, can go on endlessly. A couple may try a wide variety of different strategies over the years, discarding each in turn as it fails to get the job done. When this is the case, a good deal of friction and conflict is likely between the partners. This entire state of affairs will certainly allow the children to continue their misbehavior. It might also keep them from learning how to cope effectively with the external boundaries and limitations that they will encounter throughout the rest of their lives.

The suggestion that I am going to make for dealing with this predicament is, without a doubt, the least popular piece of advice that has ever been given in the entire history of psychology. It is the same advice I give to every couple struggling with *any* source of conflict in their relationship. I continue to trot it out, doggedly and repeatedly, despite the fact that the reaction I get is always pretty much the same: "Yech!" It's ac-

tually so unappealing that, when I try to take this advice myself, I also say "yech." Ready?

Work on the problem when you are both feeling good,
NOT when you are already arguing.

That's it. Simple and to the point. The best time for a
repartnered couple to prepare a behavioral plan of action is
during the initial disciplinary honeymoon, not when things are
already in the midst of unraveling. If you don't get such a honeymoon period, then you should start working on your program right away, but only at times when both you and your
partner are in a good mood.

How much progress can be made on these difficult issues when everyone is already angry, pressured, frustrated,
and defensive? None. None at all. The oft-photocopied
proverb that appears in so many business offices goes directly to this point: "It's hard to remember when you're up to
your ass in alligators that your original job was to drain the
swamp." (Similarly, couples who quarrel repeatedly about
the same subjects should consider discussing them at a time
when they are not already fighting. Follow this advice and put
me out of business.)

The problem with this advice is that nobody, including
me, wants to risk destroying a perfectly good mood by discussing things that have a history of leading directly to upset.
Most of us have learned the hard way that talking about conflict often leads to conflict. The fact is that this doesn't always
have to be the case.

In order to prevent flare-ups while discussing difficult
topics, couples should establish some rules ahead of time.
For example, it can be agreed upon that an emotional subject
will be dropped as soon as the interaction becomes too
heated. There is no dishonor in this type of strategic retreat.
After all, you are not trying to win, you are trying to discuss. A
previous, more pleasant activity should then be resumed,

with the understanding that another approach will be made to the troublesome topic sometime in the immediate future. As difficult and potentially unpleasant as this sounds, it is the only way that I know of for couples to make meaningful progress toward resolving their conflicts. Could this be yet another one of those times when good wine and candlelight might be helpful?

Given the opportunity, parents in stepfamilies should develop their behavioral program when things are calm, well before the alligators arrive. If you are lucky enough to have a disciplinary honeymoon period, you and your partner should have enough time to negotiate and compromise without too much difficulty at all. If those nasty, crocodilian reptiles are already in the swamp, then do the necessary work at those times when you are not already angry about what the kids did and how your partner managed to mishandle it. The long-term, positive results that you will eventually obtain are well worth your taking the risk that a few good moods might go bad. Honest!

The final benefit that the behavioral program can provide to a repartnered couple is help in dealing with one or two ex-partners who might have hostile feelings toward the new family. As mentioned previously, if all of the involved parents are mutually supportive regarding the way that discipline is handled in the various households, you have arrived in behavioral heaven. If one or more of the grown-ups appear to be working against such an ideal situation, however, the program can provide a strong, formal framework with which to counterbalance any such negative influences. This system, when it is consistently applied, will bring about behavioral improvement in your home regardless of the ex-partners' attitudes toward the blended family. The children need to know that rules will be enforced in your household despite the fact that conditions might be entirely different when they are with their other parents. Although this is not the perfect situation, it is most certainly better than allowing ex-partners to generate conflict within the new family.

THE DISNEYLAND PARENT

First, in a direct attempt to avoid the kind of prolonged and costly litigation about trade name infringement that I would surely lose in the end, I want to stress that my use of the phrase "Disneyland Parent" is not intended to imply anything the least bit negative about the late Walt Disney, his theme parks, or his mouse friend. Quite the contrary. I have used this phrase for years to describe a style of parenting that is sometimes exploited by the ex-partner who has less custody of the children.

This parent attempts to assure a positive relationship with the kids, and to compensate for the loss of time together, by constantly providing them with the emotional equivalent of Disneyland. While theme parks are certainly great places to visit, they are not necessarily the best places to live. Disneyland Parents may accomplish the goal of developing a highly positive bond with their children, but it is usually at the cost of causing tremendous difficulties in the other parent's household. Additionally, the problems that this approach might later cause the children can be profound.

When I was a child, my allegiance having long since been sworn to *The Mickey Mouse Club,* I expected that my soul would ascend directly to Disneyland upon my demise. Here was an ideal world where dreams really came true, a perfect land of amusement rides, parades, endless play, and fantasy. I don't think that Walt, himself, would have been unhappy with my perception. It makes complete sense to me that parents would want to give their children Disneyland, or all that is most wonderful in life, while trying to spare them from any emotional upset. This should be a basic part of the job description for parenting. On the other hand, the idea that parents can actually provide their children with all of the good while protecting them for all of the bad is truly a fantasy. At Disneyland, you have to pay on the way in, and they make sure that you leave at the end of the day. It is a given that this perfect world is a "Fantasyland."

The Disneyland Parent tends to shy away from any disciplinary approach that could cause conflict with the children. Kids don't generally have to be brought back into line if they are constantly entertained, taken places, and given things. When a couple divorces, usually only the less custodial parent is in a position to take this kind of approach. Any ongoing behavioral problems that the children have can safely be ignored since, with the limited time usually shared between this parent and the kids, such difficulties will likely appear only in the more custodial household. The strategy of giving the children everything they want while ignoring their negative behaviors can be very effective in maintaining unruffled relationships. When one parent uses this approach, the other is left to deal with the behavioral disaster that quite frequently develops.

The parent who does not have the luxury to take the Disneyland approach is placed in a very difficult situation by the one who does. In Chapter 1, I said that parents must set limits as a way of teaching their children about the real boundaries in the adult world. When children are given what they need rather than all that they want, and when they see consistent consequences for good and bad behavior, then they will learn to satisfy their needs in socially acceptable ways. On the other hand, kids who are always given the Disneyland treatment might never get the hang of these vitally important lessons.

A confusing, mixed message is often sent to children who spend some of their time in a household with clearly defined boundaries, and some of their time with a Disneyland Parent. It is certainly not a surprise that many of these kids express a preference for the latter. (Some children, especially when they are older, can see through this type of superficial relationship.) This can be quite hurtful and frustrating to a single or repartnered parent who is trying to raise the type of children who will develop into socially responsible adults.

If you are raising children by yourself, you certainly don't need me to tell you that this can be a very difficult undertaking. Similarly, if you have formed a stepfamily, you are already aware of the pitfalls, confusions, and conflicts that can develop. When your child-rearing situation is complicated by an estranged, Disneyland Parent, however, there are some things that we need to talk about. Single or divorced parenting is hard enough without this additional distraction.

The most common parental complaint that I hear in this circumstance is that children view the more custodial parent as an ogre in comparison to the Disneyland Parent. If you are enforcing rules for behavior in your household, no matter how benign or appropriate, the kids might try to exploit your ex-partner's laxness as a weapon in their battle for complete freedom. There is a good chance that you will become sick-to-death of hearing that: 1) your ex-partner doesn't make them do that, 2) they're going to tell your ex-partner that you make them do that, 3) they'd rather live with your ex-partner, and, most devastating, 4) they like your ex-partner better than they like you. Stepparents might also look forward to being on the receiving end of some very sharp barbs.

Don't give in to this nonsense. You are doing the right thing, and the Disneyland Parent is definitely not. There are a number of reasons for my emphasis here, but the first and most important fact for you to keep in mind is that the children are still primarily living with *you*. If they were really so sure that the other parent was providing a healthier environment for their development, they would struggle relentlessly to leave your household. When that is the case, consideration should be given to the possibility that a change in the custody arrangements could be beneficial to everyone involved. Otherwise, you can be fairly certain that the kids are just using the Disneyland Parent in their attempts to avoid any discipline at all. I continue to be impressed by the fact that these children almost always refuse my offer to arrange for them to live with their Disneyland Parent. What does this mean?

This means that children actually want their parents to be in control. As I mentioned in Chapter 1, kids will never directly tell you that they want and need the limits that you are supposed to provide. Instead, they will gladly accept any power over household events that their parents let them have. Testing the limits of a parent's authority is a critical developmental task for children. It is extremely important that they be able to find these boundaries.

Many kids are not consciously aware of their need for parental guidance. Even those who are will only infrequently admit that they could benefit in any way from such restrictions. The problem here is the tremendous confusion that can develop for children who are never sure of whether, or how, their parents might respond to particular behaviors. This situation alone can lead to the display of a wide variety of negative behaviors on the part of the children.

No one would argue with the fact that there is trouble ahead for custodial parents who always let the children have their way. Kids in this circumstance will learn nothing about life in the real world, and, because their judgmental skills are not yet fully developed, they will also make their parents completely miserable. Disneyland Parents can take this approach only because of the limited amount of time that they spend with the children and because any behavioral problems that the children develop will show up primarily in the more custodial household.

The situation is even worse for those parents who usually let the children do anything they want but who occasionally lay down the law in no uncertain terms. This completely inconsistent approach to discipline is guaranteed to confuse everyone in the household, and to result in extremely negative behavior from the kids. What constitutes proper behavior becomes a total mystery to children who can never be sure of how their parents will respond to a given situation.

I am convinced that almost all children have some level of awareness that it is their parents who are supposed to be in control. I also believe that, despite anything they say or do to demonstrate the contrary, they are generally more comfortable when the expectations and consequences for behavior are completely clear. As a divorced or single parent with an ex-partner who has become a Disneyland Parent, you are still absolutely right to establish a well-defined, behavioral program like the one described in this book. The presence of the Disneyland Parent only serves to make this type of approach even more important. Chaos is usually the result if no one in a child's life provides a sensible level of discipline.

By definition, the Disneyland Parent will avoid the type of discipline that could lead to conflict with the kids. If you are tempted to enter into a "Best Disneyland Parent" competition with your ex-partner in order to "buy" your children's affection and cooperation, the end result will surely be a calamity. Your job is to develop a unified and consistent approach to discipline in your home even if you seem to be losing a popularity contest to the other parent.

Perhaps you can convince your ex-partner that the Disneyland approach does more harm than good. Perhaps not. As the more custodial parent, your approach to discipline will have a positive influence on the children no matter what is happening in the other household. You may have to listen to complaints and unflattering comparisons from the children, but *you are doing the right thing*. Again, although they might not admit it, kids have a "deep-down" understanding of the fact that they need the limits and boundaries that good parents provide. My experience has been that children will ultimately accept, if not welcome, such guidance. They may go kicking and screaming every inch of the way, but they'll go. Someday, they may even understand that the Disneyland Parent's approach was never in their best interests.

If you are very, very lucky, the time may come when your children will thank you for giving them the clear, unified, and consistent parenting that allowed them to develop to their maximum potential. They might not get this idea until they are raising their own children. They might never get it. If that's the case, you should still always be proud of the fact that you took on an extremely difficult job, by yourself or with a new partner, and that you did it the right way.

CHAPTER 9

School-Based Programs

Hello, school personnel. This chapter is just for you. Everyone else can skip on to Chapter 10, "Three Case Studies." School folks get their own chapter for several reasons. First, since kids spend so much of their time there, schools are in an ideal position to help improve children's behavior. Second, when even one child's behavior is uncontrolled, entire classrooms can be disrupted. Third, teachers need a straightforward and effective approach to improving behavior so that they can devote more of their limited time to teaching. Fourth, a structured program can help children with special problems, such as ADHD or Tourette's disorder, to control their behavior and increase the educational benefit of their classroom time. Finally, the improvement in a child's behavior is maximized when the same approach is used at home and in school. This program is an effective way to help school children of all ages.

So, the good news is that you get a chapter of your own about applying this method in school. The bad news is that you still have to read everything we've covered up to this point. You can't just skip to this part in order to get the gist of the school-based program. The structure and operation are the same whether the system is applied in school or at home. The only differences are that the Target Goals, Rewards, and Penalties are specific to the school environment and that other school personnel may be involved in designing, implementing, and communicating about the program.

If you are the only teacher with whom the child in question has contact, or if you are the only one for whom the child is misbehaving, you can work alone in designing the school-based program. If the child's behavior is causing problems for other teachers, however, it is best to have them participate in the design as well. You might also want to include members of the school's guidance, psychology, or social work staffs.

Everything that has been said about how couples should work together on this project also applies to groups of school folks. For the program to be most effective, it must be applied consistently throughout the school day by the different people who are having difficulty with the child. If the design tasks are shared by all of the professionals who have contact with the child, everyone's concerns can be represented in the finished program. Further, all involved staff members will have an in-depth understanding of how to apply the system. When the staff shares all of the information about how the program is running, consistency will be maintained and the child won't "slip through the cracks." It also becomes much harder for a child to exploit one teacher's lack of knowledge about what is going on in another's classroom, playing teacher against teacher, if these teachers are regularly discussing the child. Loopholes that might allow children to manipulate the existing disciplinary approach can be closed through ongoing communication about this program.

It is relatively easy to run this program in a single classroom. If different teachers are using the same approach with the same child, however, I advise that they not each design their own program. It would be much too hard for a child to keep track of the variety of different Target Goals, Rewards, and Penalties that would exist between several classrooms. Rather, a single system that is consistent throughout the child's day should be designed by the involved staff members.

TARGET GOALS AND
OPERATIONAL DEFINITION

The process of generating Target Goals for school is exactly the same as that for the home. Everyone participating in the design should work together to generate a "wish list" of behaviors that need to be started and those that need to be stopped. Include chores only if they are appropriate for your classroom. As mentioned in Chapter 2, anything goes at this stage. If there are differences of opinion between staff members, include the items for later discussion.

I have no doubt that you are painfully aware of the many problems that might become the basis for Target Goals in school. Here's a sample list of some very popular items:

1. He (or she, throughout) should not be wandering in the halls, especially with a bathroom pass.
2. No hitting.
3. He should keep his nose out of others' business. He shouldn't get involved when a teacher is disciplining another student. He does this even when he's directly told not to.
4. He should stop lying when he's caught doing something wrong. This happens even when a teacher actually sees him misbehave.
5. He should do his classroom work on time.
6. He should get to the right places at the right times.
7. His interactions with the other children should be more appropriate.
8. He should do his homework. Then, he should turn it in.
9. He should bring the required materials, such as pencils, pens, books, and art materials, to class.
10. He should be more involved with the other students instead of being so isolated.
11 . He should not speak out in class unless he has permission.

Pretty familiar stuff, no? With a little bit of work, all of these items can become solid Target Goals. Other Goals might include such things as following directions and staying seated. Remember that the Goals must involve behavior rather than attitude.

The next step, of course, is to develop operational definitions for the items on the original Target Goals list. Courtesy of our friends from the earlier chapters, Bryan and Derek, you should already be an old hand at this. Here is an item-by-item discussion of some things to be considered in operationally defining each of the Goals mentioned above:

1. He should not be in the hall *at all* without a pass. How many bathroom passes should he have during each class or each day? How long should he be out of class with a pass?

2. No hitting. No hitting back. This Goal should always reflect your school's policy on fighting.

3. If a child often "butts into" situations inappropriately, a specific Goal can be written to address this. If it is an infrequent occurrence, the Three-Time Rule is the most effective tool to use. Yes, I add the Three-Time Rule to all school-based programs.

4. In school, as well as at home, a child can be penalized for lying only when caught. The staff member is the final judge as to whether there's been a lie. If later evidence shows that a mistake has been made, the consequences can be changed accordingly after the involved school personnel discuss the situation.

5. How many times should the child be told to do classwork? How much work should be done? By what time should it be done? Should this be judged by the quantity of work or by the amount of time spent doing it? It's not easy being a teacher.

6. What room, what time, what bell, what pass?

7. What is he doing that's not appropriate? Usually, this involves verbal abuse or hitting. We already took care of the hitting. You'll have to define verbal abuse.

8. He should present his homework when asked. How much homework? All the homework. Teachers, as well as parents, can initiate the use of a Home/School Homework Log, as described in Chapter 3. This must always be a cooperative effort between the home and the school.

9. He should bring the necessary equipment. How much equipment? All the equipment.

10. Describe what you want the child to do (play in a group, for example), when and how it should be done, and who will be keeping track of it. Easy.

11. He should not speak out in class unless this is generally allowed. Does he get one or more warnings? Does waving his hands while squirming around and making "uh, uh, uh, memememe" noises count as speaking out? If speaking out on the topic at hand is acceptable, but socializing isn't, the Goal must be written accordingly.

12. This is where you would add the Three-Time Rule. It is just as important in school as it is at home. Of course.

The number of Goals in the school-based program should be lower than it would be at home, perhaps five or less. There is already enough to keep track of in the classroom without adding unnecessary complication. You can always drop or combine Goals if necessary.

REWARDS AND PENALTIES

This is the part where school folks have to be at their most creative. You know the kids in your classes and what they will respond to. I can tell you some of the things that other teachers have suggested, but you'll have to find the consequences that matter to a given child. Nobody said this was going to be easy. At least it's only a five-day week.

For a young child, the Reward can be as simple as a sticker given on each day that all the Goals are accomplished. This is only effective if stickers are important to the child. Remember that the daily Reward must have enough value to justify the child's working for it. It should also be something tangible that the child can take and keep. When I presented this program to some teachers in my community, I was told that pencils remain a very solid choice for the elementary school set. Unusual pencils are even better. I think that video games are neat, but it was refreshing to hear that "low-tech" is still holding its own.

Tokens or coupons can be used with children of all ages. The tokens must have a prearranged value, and the child must be able to use them to buy prizes (items or privileges) with given costs. Play money is always useful for this. Like other Rewards, tokens should not be taken back as a Penalty once they are given. The prizes that kids can get with tokens should not be confused with the Bonus Reward. The Bonus is given only after a perfect week. Prizes can be bought whenever the child has enough tokens.

The most popular school-based Reward of all time, of course, is homework reduction. This can be a daily Reward, the Bonus for a perfect week, or a prize to be bought with tokens. Most of the items that make good Bonuses can also be used as prizes. Children will work toward extra recess, art, or gym; playtime with toys, clay, or computers; items from the school store; or special recognition in the classroom. Did I mention that they are often interested in reducing the amount of their homework?

The Big Bonus, coming after four to six weeks of perfect (or close to it) performance, should have great value or honor attached to it. Teachers of younger children have told me that having a special breakfast or lunch with a child can be a wonderful

Reward. Teachers of older kids have pointed out that this same consequence might be considered slightly more punishing than the tortures of hell. You can always use larger versions of the weekly Bonus Rewards. Or *dozens* of pencils. Be creative.

In the Penalty department, teachers often mention the usefulness of mild social isolation. The best example of this approach would be to reduce recess time for younger children. Older kids might lose time in a favored, elective class. If necessary, children can be physically isolated within a classroom or sent to the school office or to a "detention" room for a specified time period. The idea of these Penalties is not to embarrass a child in front of peers but to remove that child from "where the action is." As in the home-based program, Penalties should involve elapsed time. Rather than just taking away an entire recess for an infraction, for example, you would subtract a given amount of time from recess for each missed Goal. This Penalty time would add to that for mistakes on the preceding or following days, just as described in Chapter 5, until the child achieved a perfect day.

You may feel uncomfortable in carrying over and adding to the consequences from a previous day. Some teachers prefer to address each day's disciplinary events on that day only. I have noticed, though, that the consequences for some of *my* behaviors have lasted *far* longer than one day. The carryover of Penalty time is designed to get kids back on track quickly and is an integral part of this approach.

THE PROGRAM

The first item to consider is whether parents need to be notified that this program will be used to help their children in the classroom. Some school systems have distinct policies about this. There are several reasons why I always recommend that parents be informed about the program. Parents need to know about the behavioral difficulties that you are having with their children and what you are doing to address these problems. Since the child is going to be talking about the program at home, the parents will need enough information to understand what is taking place. Parental support for this school-based approach is invaluable in making it successful. Finally, parents may want to design a similar program to be used when the child is at home.

Next is the Chart (as if I would need to tell *teachers* anything about how to make a chart). Make a Chart.

The daily communication period described in Chapter 6 applies here as well, but there might be more people involved. If you are the only one running the program, you can keep your own counsel. This should be approached as if you were a single parent (as described in Chapter 8). If you have assistants in your room, or if you are one of several teachers who will be running the program, you will all need to talk each day about the Chart. You can make the discussion brief if things are running well, but, at the very least, you must all "touch base" about the children in question. This may seem like a lot of work, but there will be a big payoff in improved behavior. You are already spending large amounts of time on dealing with these problems. Overall, there will be less work if you do it together and focus your energy.

The rest of the program is the same as that which is run by parents. The Three-Time Rule and Time-Outs should be used in the same ways. You will need to show the same enthusiasm in approaching the children. The same decisions will have to be made about whether or not to give prompts, whether fine-tuning is required, and so forth.

A QUICK EXAMPLE

Mary has five Target Goals. Every day that she accomplishes all five Goals, she receives a coupon. Each daily coupon can be redeemed for the subtraction of one item from her homework.

If she has a perfect week, she gets a Bonus of thirty extra minutes of computer time on the following Monday. Because she earned it in the previous week, she gets this Bonus time even if Monday is not perfect. When she has a perfect month, she becomes the Superintendent of Schools. No, no, no. Just kidding! How about a special lunch with her teacher? For a missed item, Mary loses ten minutes of recess time as well as her Bonus and Big Bonus Rewards (although the flexibility in the Big Bonus that was discussed in Chapter 5 should apply in school, as well). The recess penalty will continue to add up until Mary has a perfect day, at which time her recess returns to its full length.

There's the bell! It's time to return to your classrooms. Good luck!

CHAPTER 10

Three Case Studies

Unlike Bryan and Derek, our hypothetical children, the kids described in this chapter are very real. Although their identities have been disguised, their stories come directly from my notes. These three cases demonstrate the wide range of behaviors, for children of varying ages, that can be improved with this program. Of course, the real reason that they are here is because the case studies are always my favorite part of books like this one. You will be mercifully spared the painful ordeal of going through any more operational definitions!

SARAH

Sarah was fourteen years old when she first came to see me. She had been very depressed, angry, and suicidal. Sarah admitted that she had often carved on her wrists and arms before her parents sent her to a psychiatric hospital for several weeks. There had been several recent deaths, as well as other legal and medical problems, in her extended family. Although these events were clearly quite stressful for her, she was most concerned with the possibility that her parents would get a divorce. In the course of our work together, Sarah acknowledged that much of her negative behavior at home and in school was related to her feelings about the divorce. She expressed her fear and anger by refusing to accept others' authority over her. Violations of curfew, refusals to do school work, lies, and minor household thefts were common.

Sarah was able to come to terms with her feelings after a year of individual and family psychotherapy. Her depression lifted and she was able to express her emotions directly through words. She was then able to deal more effectively with the fact that her parents had decided to proceed with the divorce.

Much of Sarah's negative behavior had also improved through the process of psychotherapy, but there were still several problems. Her parents and I decided that a structured approach to behavioral change was appropriate at that time. Sarah's mom and dad constructed a list of Target Goals, which we then narrowed and operationally defined. Here is the final version:

1. She will not lie when caught in misbehavior. This includes lies of omission ("I didn't know that I should tell you *that. . .*") as well as lies of commission ("I didn't do it").

2. Sarah will do all homework assignments, every night, for not less than two hours. She will present a Home/School Homework Log, including advance notice of assignments and tests, to her parents and to all of her teachers every day.

3. She will not take or use other family members' belongings without permission or allow her friends to do the same. She will not give her friends access to parts of the house that her parents declare off-limits (such as their bedroom).

4. No making firm recreational plans without parental permission. No riding in others' cars without permission.

5. Sarah will clean her room and bathroom on Thursday, removing clothes and other items from the floors, before bedtime. She will make her bed each day.

6. She will not wear her street clothes to bed. (Honest!)

7. Bedtime will be 10:30 P.M. on school days, 11:30 on weekends during the school year, and 11:30 in the summer unless prior arrangements have been made. Wake up time will be 6:15 A.M. during the school year.

8. Specified pool maintenance will be done by 6:00 P.M. daily in the summer. Sarah will do minor household and yard chores, without complaint, at either parent's request. The cat's litter box will be scooped daily and changed every third day (according to a chart).

9. The Three-Time Rule (of course).

Sarah's parents decided that her Reward would be an allowance of $21.00 per week, or $3.00 per day. For her Bonus Reward, she would be allowed to choose between $5.00, one hour of curfew extension on one day, or half an hour of curfew extension on each of two days. Her Big Bonus Reward, given after a perfect month, would be $30.00 or a one month membership in a local health club (a roughly equivalent amount). The Penalty was nasty for a fourteen-year-old girl: a one hour restriction from telephone use. A Time-Out period of fifteen minutes was selected. Sarah and her parents frequently worked together on the design of the program.

As a result of scheduling difficulties, the family and I were not able to meet for twelve days after the start of the program. At that time, they reported that Sarah had had eleven perfect days and only one miss. The Penalty occurred when she didn't do one of her chores, a rather minor error in light of what had brought them to my office in the first place. The family was thrilled with the overall reduction in conflict that had taken place as a result of the program. I emphasized both Sarah's individual accomplishments and the positive effect it was having on her relationship with her parents. No fine-tuning was necessary.

When they ultimately divorced, Sarah's parents successfully and uneventfully continued to run the program in each household. Sarah and I were then able to focus our attention on some difficulties that she had been having in her relationships with other people. Treatment was completed and the case was closed six months later.

MATT

Matt was a very angry eight-year-old boy when I first met him. He had had some suicidal thoughts a year earlier, but things had been relatively calm since then. Now, he was again talking about hurting himself or his six-year-old brother, Greg. His behavior at home was terrible, complete with screaming, door slamming, and wall banging. Matt absolutely refused to obey his mother, who was attempting to complete her college education while working full-time as well. There were tremendous arguments between mother and son, resulting in frequent telephone calls to Matt's father, a retail salesperson. Both parents complained of being unable to focus on their work because of the upset at home. They felt that Matt was ruining their lives. The father had developed some resentment about coming home each night and being expected to discipline Matt immediately for things that had taken place during the day.

After several weeks of talking to Matt and his family, I believed that we had uncovered the roots of his anger and negative behavior. First, Matt felt that his parents favored his brother so much that they wouldn't listen to his side of any story. He presented compelling evidence that he was often blamed for situations that Greg had caused, and that Greg was regularly allowed to escape punishment. Since I hear so much of this kind of thing from kids with brothers and sisters, I always do a bit more digging before jumping to conclusions. I shared Matt's concerns with his parents. They agreed to monitor their children's interactions more closely in order to collect additional information. The surprise came when they reported that Matt had been right. His brother had been teasing him and inciting him to misbehave. Matt would be caught, Greg would leave the scene, and Matt would be punished. His parents immediately took steps to put this situation in balance and to listen more carefully to Matt's complaints.

Next, it appeared unlikely that Matt's parents could have been any less unified and consistent in their approach to discipline. Because of their frustration with Matt's oppositional and defiant behaviors, they had become overly harsh in their punishments. His mother had read every available book on child behavior and had tried everything. She had found little help and was left shouting, grounding, and threatening that dad would come home from work and really punish Matt. Matt's father, of course, hated to come home to his role as "The Enforcer." He realized that he could not have a positive relationship with his son if they were always in conflict as soon as he walked through the door. The only choices that he felt were left to him were to spank or to threaten spankings. In the heat of battle, Matt's father was also known to threaten punishments that were much too severe for the problem at hand. He was tired of the telephone calls at work, and he wanted his wife to handle discipline during the day.

Matt's parents admitted that they didn't always agree with each other's disciplinary style. Worse, they acknowledged that they sometimes actively undermined each other, arguing loudly in front of Matt about what the other parent should have done. Although they constantly talked about this situation, which had entirely taken over their lives, they had been unable to improve it. It sounded like a job for a structured and consistent behavioral program.

Matt's parents came up with this operationally defined list of Target Goals:

1. Matt will make his bed, brush his teeth, and dress himself by 8:30 A.M. daily.
2. He will receive no negative behavior reports from school.

3. His homework must be completely done by dinnertime.
4. Matt will clear the table every night immediately after dinner.
5. He will pick up in his room, put his dirty clothes in the hamper, and brush his teeth before bedtime at 8:00 P.M.
6. He will not throw or break things when he is angry and/or frustrated.
7. Matt will not tattle on his brother when what Greg is doing does not directly involve him. This does not include situations in which Greg might be in actual danger.
8. He will put away items from one activity before starting another.
9. He will not hit his brother.
10. The Three-Time Rule.

Matt's Reward was set at $5.25 per week, or 75¢ per day. His Bonus Reward was four packs of baseball cards or $2.00 in cash. His Big Bonus Reward, for one month of perfect performance, was a Radio Shack electronics kit in the $15 to $20 range, or the equivalent amount of cash. His Penalty was the ever-popular early bedtime, in ten-minute slices. Time- Outs were to be ten minutes long as well. Matt's parents also designed a similar program for his brother. At the point where both Charts were constructed and ready to go, they informed me that they were: 1) fed up with Matt, 2) skeptical about the program, and 3) angry at everyone (including me) for everything. My kind of challenge.

Matt's folks were still angry after the program had been running for a week. Although he had had a perfect week, his dad was focused on punishing negative behaviors that weren't included on the Chart. We discussed the idea that traditional penalties, such as restriction of Matt's privileges or being sent to his room, might be appropriate for occasional misbehavior that was not included in the program. We also went over the Three-Time Rule. Mom had gotten into a power struggle with Matt over the time that he should make his bed. She wanted it to be done by the same deadline throughout the week. Matt wanted more flexibility on weekends. I said that the parents should discuss this during their nightly communication period in order to reach a unified decision. They did, and Matt was given special dispensation (a later deadline) on weekends.

It saddened me that Matt's parents had become so immersed in the details of the program that they were not expressing any pride in his perfect week. I pointed this out to them and then met with Matt privately. I praised him for going a full week without hitting his brother, a new world's record. He was pleased with his allowance and with my appreciation of his newly improved behavior.

Matt had one miss the following week, and then he put together a perfect month. He went for the cash Big Bonus and became independently wealthy. His parents were very happy with the positive changes in Matt and in the household. They became much more free with their praise when they saw how well he responded to it. They were not so thrilled to find that, without Matt's misbehavior to argue about and focus on, marital problems that they had ignored for years now resurfaced with a vengeance. Stresses on the marriage then became the main subject in sessions with the couple. Matt's program required only minor fine-tuning before the case was successfully closed. The family stayed intact and Matt no longer reported experiencing any suicidal feelings.

DOUG

Our last case is that of Doug, an eleven-year-old boy whose older sister had been tragically killed in a boating accident two years earlier. This event continued to exert a huge influence on Doug's relationship with his parents. His sister had been a highly gifted student and athlete for whom major accomplishments came very easily. His parents wanted Doug to achieve this same level of success despite the fact that he did not share his sister's gifts. Doug felt that he was competing with his dead sister for his parents' attention. He also felt that he could never measure up to his sister's achievements.

Quite understandably, Doug's parents had become overprotective of him. This took the form of their being overly strict and rigid in discipline. Doug responded with bouts of anger. He engaged his parents in frequent struggles over his bedtime schedule and household chores, and he would always procrastinate. His continual exhaustion in school and declining grades indicated that, although Doug frequently won these battles, he was losing the war.

Many sessions were spent on working to resolve the family's difficulties in dealing with the sister's death. Doug's parents began to focus more on their living child than on the one who had been lost. There were discussions about the fine line between protecting and overprotecting a child. Since the entire family wanted to stop the constant fighting over Doug's schedules and responsibilities, we decided to design a behavioral program in order to establish clear guidelines. Here are the ten final Target Goals that resulted:

1. Doug will not mock his parents. Mocking is defined as attempting to ridicule them through imitation.
2. He will not immediately yell "no" in response to his parents' requests. He will discuss his objections calmly.
3. He will not sneak out of bed to watch TV.
4. Doug will respond within thirty seconds when called by his parents. This will only apply when they are in the same room with him or when they can directly see him.

5. He will clear the table after all meals. When the family has company, he will help clean up until he is dismissed by his parents.
6. He will provide food and water for the dog before breakfast. He will walk and brush the dog each afternoon before dinner.
7. Doug will pick up items from the floor of his room by bedtime.
8. He will take the garbage cans to the curb on Fridays by 3:30 P.M.
9. He will do house or yard chores, at either parent's request, for a maximum of one hour per day and two hours per week.
10. The Three-Time Rule.

Doug's parents decided that he would receive an allowance of $5.25 per week, or 75¢ per day, for perfect performance. His Bonus Reward was a videocassette rental of his choice or $2.50 in cash. The Big Bonus Reward, after six weeks of perfection, was a day trip of his choice. A bedtime Penalty of fifteen minutes and a Time-Out period of ten minutes were chosen.

Doug had a three-day trial run before the program started in earnest. The first day did not go at all well, with several misses and a good deal of arguing about the system. This was followed by two perfect days and a regularly scheduled family session at my office. We discussed who got to decide whether a Goal was correctly accomplished (either parent), who assigned yard and household chores (either parent), how the parents should decide on which chores were to be assigned (communication), and whether Doug should be the one to choose which chores he would and would not do (no).

Doug had a single miss during the next week. He violated his first Target Goal with a big outburst of mocking when he disagreed with his parents. The Penalty was invoked and the behavior was not repeated that week. Doug's parents were satisfied that they now had the tools needed to help him improve his behavior. Since the goals of our work together had been reached, the case was closed with the understanding that they could always call me with any questions about the program. That call never came, which I took to be a very good sign.

*T*roubleshooting

Here's a chapter that sounds like it belongs in the repair manual for a car or a major appliance. Troubleshooting always comes near the very end of the book. It's the part that tells you what to do when you've followed all of the other directions, but things still aren't working the way that they're supposed to. You're generally told to start with the most obvious ("Is it plugged in?") and work your way toward the most serious ("The telephone number for our supplier in Northern Siberia is . . ."). You are also usually made to believe that the problem was caused by something that you did wrong. Since children have neither plugs nor Northern Siberian suppliers (except, of course, Northern Siberian children), how does troubleshooting apply to them? As you might guess, my approach to this is going to be a little bit different than the standard checklist of possible mechanical malfunctions. For example, I believe that you could still end up with a disciplinary problem even if you have perfectly carried out every bit of advice in this book.

Although it wounds my pride even to mention it, there is always the possibility that the behavioral program I have described has not worked for you. There are several reasons why this might happen. We will review some of the problems in designing and running this program that can lead to its failure. I will also make the case that no matter how careful your work on the system, there are some children who will just not respond to it. The possible explanations for this situation will be examined and, more importantly, recommendations will be made about what can be done when all else has failed. Remember, if what you are doing isn't working after you have given it a fair trial, it's time to stop doing it and try something else. That advice also applies to (shudder) this behavioral program.

SO, WHAT COULD GO WRONG?

TOGETHERNESS AND COMMUNICATION

Despite the fact that there is little in the world that is more boring than listening to someone beat the proverbial dead horse, I'm going to make sure that there is not a trace of life left in that poor old beast. There are several steps in the construction of the program that, when omitted or modified, can be counted upon to cause the whole thing to self-destruct. Since I trust that you are reading this entire book before starting to design your own program (as I recommended in the Preface), these warnings will serve as another reminder about the most important points in the procedure. If you are rereading this chapter because problems developed while you were actually running the system, then this is the place to start your troubleshooting.

We will begin by returning to that innocent time when I first asked you to make lists of your Target Goals, Rewards, and Penalties. Can you sense what's coming? Yes, it's that if you are part of a couple that is living together, *you must sit down TOGETHER and construct these lists TOGETHER!* I believe I may have mentioned that through trial and error, it became very clear that when only one parent in a couple constructs the lists and the other parent just checks, edits, or accepts them, absolute failure is absolutely guaranteed. *Do it TOGETHER!* In Chapter 2, I said that the list project provided an accurate barometer of a couple's commitment to working on the behavioral program. Just as crucial is the fact that each parent must be thoroughly familiar with every aspect of this system, from start to finish. At the most basic level, this prevents the time-consuming repetition that results when one partner is constantly trying to catch up with what the other has done. It also allows couples to avoid the situation in which one parent is viewed by the other as the architect of the system and, therefore, as the primary disciplinarian.

As mentioned in Chapter 1, the fact that disciplinary authority is to be equally shared by the parents is of the greatest importance. Each partner must be fully invested in this approach in order to feel positive about using it. That can never be the case if both parents are not totally involved as the program is designed and implemented. When each parent is contributing to the system from the beginning, and when each of their disciplinary styles is represented in the final product, the result will be a shared level of enthusiasm and commitment. There is little chance that this approach can succeed if one partner is being dragged along, willingly or unwillingly, by the other.

While it is very important for the parents to view themselves as equal partners in providing discipline, it is even more necessary for their children to perceive them as completely interchangeable (as discussed in Chapters 1, 4, 6, and 8). For this system to be effective, both parents must provide exactly the same Rewards and Penalties, at the same times and in the same ways, for the list of Target Goals. Children quickly develop expertise at playing their mother and father against each other. They learn to exploit the fact that parents generally can't communicate with each other about every single child-rearing decision. "But *Mom* said" and "But *Dad* said" are surely near the top of the "Most Frequently Heard Childhood Whines" list.

In order to close this loophole, parents must make sure that they each have the same expectations for their children's behavior, and that the consequences for this behavior will always be the same. The easiest way to ensure such consistency and unity is for the partners to work _together_ in constructing the lists of Target Goals, Rewards, and Penalties. The quickest way for parents to bring about the failure of this system is to work as individuals rather than as a team. Spend all of the time that's necessary to do a thorough job on the initial assignment. If you have run the program without having constructed the lists together, and if you have not gotten positive results, I recommend that you start the whole thing again from the beginning. I believe that I can now pronounce this particular horse to be officially dead.

There is a second element directly related to the first, that will completely defeat this approach to helping your difficult child behave if it is omited. It is, of course, the communication period. Did you see this one coming? I recall using a few italics in Chapter 6 when I said that _the daily communication period is by far the most important part of this whole program. Nothing else in the program will work if it is ignored. This level of communication must continue as long as the program is running, every day, without fail._ I was putting just a touch of emphasis on the idea that couples must take five or ten minutes each day to discuss everything that relates to the behavioral program.

These conversations serve a variety of purposes that are linked to the success of this method. First, just as in the construction of the original three lists, it is important that both parents be fully involved in all aspects of the program. Partners must exchange information about anything that has to do with the Chart. This level of teamwork prevents the children from exploiting any differences in the amount of information that one parent has about what the other has said and done.

Next, as you will recall, the communication period is used to get ahead of those repetitive, negative behaviors that were somehow left off the Chart. Decisions can be made about whether new Target Goals should be written or whether these problems might be addressed in some other way. It is in this fashion that you can avoid imposing the kind of inappropriate consequences that are based more on the heat of the moment than on the true requirements of the situation.

Further, the communication period is absolutely the best time to discuss such things as whether Target Goals have become outdated and need to be rewritten or eliminated. It is also when partners should talk about whether they might be undermining each other, or whether they have become truly unified and consistent in dealing with the children. Mistakes that may have been made can be examined and changes can be planned. This brief, daily period should be used to exchange every bit of available information about how the program is running and to address any problems or questions that may have come up.

The communication period is, quite simply, the single most important aspect of this entire approach to improving your children's behavior. If you leave it out, you will have done a tremendous amount of work without any possibility of getting good results. In the event that you have designed and implemented the behavioral program according to all of the recommendations *except* for the one about the daily communication period, your troubleshooting work is now over. You have found the problem. Take another look at the "Communication" section of Chapter 6, set aside the necessary time every day, and give it another try. That last, tired horse has just bitten the dust!

SO, WHAT ELSE COULD GO WRONG?

REWARDS AND PENALTIES

What if you and your partner did make the lists of Target Goals, Rewards, and Penalties together? What if you do have a daily communication period? What if you are a single parent who has faithfully followed all of the steps in designing and running the program? What if your children's behavior *still* has not improved? What else could be going wrong? As I mentioned at the beginning of this chapter, it is sometimes possible to get poor results even though you have done everything according to the book. We will first take a look at how this can happen, and then at the steps that can be taken when it does.

While this approach to helping your difficult child behave may be based on a unified and consistent parenting style, it is driven by the positive and negative consequences that are delivered to the child. No matter how much unity and consistency you bring to the project, if your children don't value the Rewards and dread the Penalties, then this system will have little effect on the way that they act. I encourage parents to consider every possibility in determining which consequences will bring about the desired results. This is the main reason that I ask them to prepare those long, original lists of potential Rewards and Penalties. If we are lucky, items taken directly from these lists will be effective when they are used in the behavioral system.

We might also be able to adjust any less-than-perfect choices so that they are appropriate for our purposes. Should our initial selections fail to do the trick, we can quickly find a more useful Reward or Penalty on the lists of potential consequences. If the program fails to improve your children's behavior even when it has been designed and run strictly according to the directions, you should start your troubleshooting with an examination of whether the consequences need to be either fine-tuned or replaced.

Before scrapping them entirely and returning to the original lists for replacements, however, I recommend that you explore ways of adjusting the consequences that you have already been using. It may require some thought, discussion, and tinkering to determine whether the Reward is too small, whether the Penalty is either too lenient or too harsh, or whether there is some problem in how the consequences are working together. Perhaps the allowance needs to be increased, or the bonuses should be made more attractive. It may be that not enough time is being subtracted from a curfew, or that so much time is being taken away for each Penalty that the result is overwhelming to the child.

I have found that, more often than not, parents' initial choices for the Rewards and Penalties are the right ones. After all, who better knows the kids' likes and dislikes than you? Who gets to hear the kids recite their likes and dislikes more often than you do? Who can stand to go through another Christmas season listening to them whining about all those likes and dislikes? Well, you're definitely stuck with it, so you might as well make the information work for you at least as well as it works for the toy manufacturers.

I advise that you begin with the most conservative approach. Start by adjusting the sizes of your consequences rather than by replacing them outright. If this doesn't do the trick, then you'll need to return to your original lists and choose another Reward, Penalty, or both. In these situations, you must first determine whether it is the positive or the negative consequences that are causing problems. It is also possible that you might have to change or replace all of them. Since children will definitely lose their enthusiasm for the program if major changes are made too often, it is important that you go very slowly and deliberately here.

Although it is rare that parents can't come up with some Reward for which a child would be willing to work, it has been known to happen. This problem is potentially fatal for the design of the behavioral program. I have encountered a few children who are not particularly interested in acquiring any more possessions or privileges than they already have (a fact that amazes those of us whose children watch television on Saturday mornings). Sometimes, this situation develops when parents provide for all of their children's wants without requiring anything from them in return. I made the point in Chapter 4 that a given Reward is only effective when a child is usually deprived of it. As we saw in Chapter 7, unless the Rewards are directly related to clear, parental expectations, kids might not be motivated toward improving their behavior. The fact is that the child who already has everything is unlikely to work for anything.

If, in your troubleshooting, you have found this to be the case, some immediate adjustments are in order. For example, you can decrease the number of expectation-free "goodies" that are usually given to your children. These have actually become rights, rather than privileges, in your household. They may need to be returned to their original status.

Such things as allowances, curfew extensions, video games, stickers, and motor vehicles are inherently rewarding to most children. In order for them to be used as tools for helping your difficult child behave, they must be tightly bound to those good old Target Goals. It is also necessary for you to limit any flow of the chosen Rewards that can come from outside of your home. With the exception of salaries for working children, you must control the presentation of the Rewards in order for them to be effective. The bad news here is that, if you have truly given your kids *everything,* and if there is no way for you to take some of it back, you will not have enough leverage to make this behavioral program successful.

There is also the possibility that you have *not* given your children everything, that you have made a clear connection between positive consequences and parental expectations, and that your kids still have absolutely no interest in whether or not they get the Rewards. For some children, there is *no* Reward that is valuable enough to cause them to make changes. They are willing to forego all of life's pleasures in order to maintain their behavioral *status quo.* There are also children who don't, or won't, value anything that their parents can provide. Some of the kids who display oppositional and defiant behaviors fall into this category. Although it is always my preference that this program be driven more by the Rewards than by the Penalties, this can't always be the case. The alternative is for you to rely primarily on stricter Penalties while you continue to use the same Rewards. Despite the fact that these negative consequences can also be undone by a number of factors, it is worth making some adjustments here before throwing in the towel and moving on to the next level of troubleshooting.

As with the Rewards, if tinkering with the size of the existing Penalty hasn't led to behavioral improvement, you should consult your original list in order to select a more effective one. It can also be helpful to use a major, off-the-Chart Reward/Penalty, such as the one about driving that was described in Chapter 7. Many of these behavioral programs have been saved by just such adjustments. Unfortunately, just as there are some children who won't respond to Rewards, there are also children who are absolutely not motivated by any Penalty.

Whether by nature or in reaction to previous punishments, some kids are able to shrug off all allowable negative consequences. When this is the case, increasing the Penalties in an attempt to fine-tune your system can lead to a dangerous situation. Some serious problems can develop from over-penalizing children, even when physical punishments aren't being used. If the Rewards are too big, you might run the risk of "spoiling" a child. If the Penalties are overly harsh, the result can be much more devastating.

Parental attention of *any* kind can be rewarding to some children. The least desirable outcome is to have kids feel rewarded through the negative attention of a Penalty. These children will then misbehave as a way of seeking their parents' attention through being penalized. This is the situation that can develop when the negative consequences far outweigh the positive, or when the Penalties are too severe. Here, again, it is important for you to make any necessary adjustments as carefully and methodically as possible.

I hope that, by this point in the chapter, you have found whatever was causing the problems in your behavioral program, made the required repairs, and been granted the gift of well-behaved children. Those of you who are in couples have worked together and communicated daily. The consequences that you had chosen were reexamined and adjusted as necessary. All's well that ends well, right? Right. If it all ended well, that is. Sometimes, even after a good deal of serious troubleshooting, problems can remain. For example, we've seen that the behavior of children who are unaffected by Rewards and Penalties will probably not be improved through this type of behavioral program. It is also possible there are other factors that are causing the system to fail. When even your troubleshooting seems to need troubleshooting, it's clearly time to call in the big guns.

SO, WHAT SHOULD I DO NOW?
CONSULTING THE PROFESSIONALS

If what you're doing isn't working after you've given it a fair trial, stop doing it and try something else. Where have I heard that before? You are reading this section because, despite your best efforts, the behavioral program has not been effective in improving your children's behavior. Has Dr. Schwarzchild done all that he could do? Has he run out of ideas? Are you going to be left, cold and alone, out in that barren wasteland of failed allowance systems? Is this the end of the line? Ha! Not by a long shot!

When the behavioral system is not sufficient to help your difficult child, the process of troubleshooting should continue, but in a different direction. The focus of further work shifts from the program itself to other ways of bringing about the desired results. There are a number of additional steps that can be taken, some of which are definitely much more appealing than others. I will be discussing a variety of possible interventions, starting with those that are the least intrusive and ending with the most serious. It is important to have an open mind when trying to determine which approach makes the most sense in dealing with very difficult behavior. There are advantages and disadvantages to each of the alternatives that I will present. Remember that even what initially appears to be an extreme option could turn out to be exactly the right one for your particular situation.

You should be able to see my first suggestion, steaming along down the tracks, from a distance of at least a couple of miles. After all, I *am* a psychologist. This should be quite familiar to you, since it could be known as "The Great, Generic, Dear Abby/Ann Landers Recommendation." I mean absolutely no disrespect by this, since the advice is always excellent. Get professional help. When the problem is too complicated to handle in the limited space of a newspaper column, these good ladies often guide us to seek the advice of experts. For psychological or behavioral difficulties, they recommend that we discuss the situation with a counselor or therapist. I hope that it doesn't appear too self-serving when I say that I couldn't agree with them more. The first logical step when you have not gotten the desired results from the behavioral program is to consult a professional.

Not just any professional will do, however. Your pediatrician or family doctor is probably not the best person for this job. It is unlikely that they have had sufficient training in dealing with the psychological and behavioral problems of children. There are, however, a large number of other academic, behavioral, and mental health specialists out there. Guidance counselors, school psychologists, nurse practitioners, social workers, psychiatrists, and psychologists are generally available in most places.

You can narrow the choices considerably by limiting your search to only those therapists and counselors who have genuine experience in working with children and their families. There are tremendous differences between providing services to adults and to children. The last thing that you want is to have a well-meaning practitioner try to approach your children as if they were just miniature grown-ups. I believe that a helping professional's title or discipline is less important than the type of experience that he or she brings to the work. Look for someone who specializes in dealing with kids and their families.

How should you go about finding such a person? Although the "Yellow Pages" of your telephone book can provide some hints, this should probably not be your only source of information in making this choice. It is always better to find out who is recommended by the people you already know and trust. Pediatricians and school personnel are usually excellent sources for referrals, as they generally have had a good deal of experience in working with the community's child and family specialists. If your child's behavioral problems are primarily school-related, talking to the school guidance counselors or social workers may be just what is needed. Other parents you know may have used therapeutic services for their children or may have heard things "through the grapevine" that could be helpful to you in your search. These folks can be the best resource of all in guiding you toward locating a competent helper.

Should such personal approaches fail, you can contact the local mental health association for a referral. Similarly, professional organizations for psychologists, psychiatrists, and social workers often provide telephone referral services. As a last resort, local advertising and the "Yellow Pages" listings under such headings as "Psychologists," "Psychiatrists," "Social Workers," and "Marriage, Family, Child, and Individual Counselors" can point you toward the child specialists in your area. Careful inquiries should be made before you consider consulting practitioners who call themselves only "psychotherapists," since they are generally not required to have any training in order to use this title.

Actually, you should make careful inquiries of and about *any* counselor or therapist you choose to consult. Find out about such things as the length of time they've been in the field, their training and experience in working with children and families, and their general approach to dealing with children's behavioral and emotional problems. These questions can be asked over the telephone or in a first office visit. You should not be timid in finding out all that you can about the credentials of the people who may become intimately involved with your family. Those framed diplomas hanging on the wall should not stop you from asking questions. I believe that it helps to have a "consumer attitude" toward these professional service providers. Each practitioner should be viewed as someone who is running a store. If one store doesn't have what you want, you should always feel free to go to another. It might pay for you to shop around until you find the right one, with the right services, at the right price.

I have often been asked how to tell whether a particular counselor is right for the job. This is always a tough question to answer because there are so many variables involved. Since no one is ever satisfied when I say that, I've come up with a fairly simple rule of thumb. If you like the chosen therapist in the first three visits, you are probably in the right place. You should most likely hang in there even if the going gets tough. After all, when you are consulting someone about difficult situations, you have to expect to encounter some bumps in the road. This is not to say that you should continue indefinitely if you are completely miserable or dissatisfied with the service being provided, but only that you should give it a fair trial.

On the other hand, if you are genuinely uncomfortable in your first visit or two, bail out and try again with another practitioner. Don't give up completely just because you assume that all therapists or counselors will take the same approach. This is definitely not the case. The next person you contact could be exactly the right one for your family. Even if you started your search in the wrong place, the things that you have learned from the experience will help you to narrow your investigation. Go to another store.

Let's say that you have now located the ideal person to help you with your troubleshooting. What should you expect in your initial visit, and how might you speed the whole process along? First, be prepared to answer a great many questions. Whether the counselor wants to start with the grown-ups, the kids, or everybody together, there will certainly be a need to exchange a lot of information. It will be your job to describe the situation that brought you in, whether in response to specific questions or as a straightforward presentation.

I always ask about the negative behaviors that the kids have been displaying and the steps that the adults have taken to deal with them. Since you are now veterans at using a comprehensive behavioral program, you should tell your therapist or counselor about the details of this system and your experiences in using it. (Personally, I think that all such helping professionals should buy their very own copy of this book, and recommend it to all of their helping professional friends. Did I mention that it's also an ideal choice for holiday giving?) The counselor will then work with you and your family to determine where the problems lie and what further steps might be taken to deal with them.

There are a number of approaches that your therapist might suggest to help bring about behavioral and emotional improvement for your child. You may be advised to pursue a single one, or to make use of some combination of treatments. For example, it might be recommended that your child be seen in individual psychotherapy, where the counselor and the child meet for a number of sessions without other family members being present. This can be the treatment of choice if it is determined that an underlying depression or anxiety is having a negative impact on the child's behavior.

Another possibility is that family therapy might be suggested. In this approach, different combinations of family members work with the therapist at different times. It is even possible that couples or marital therapy could be recommended. This can be quite an effective approach when a child is reacting negatively to either a couple's lack of unity and consistency in discipline, or to struggles within that couple's relationship. In this type of situation, I have sometimes been able to help improve a child's behavior while doing very little direct work with the child at all. Resolving the couple's difficulties, or helping them to develop a coherent disciplinary strategy, is often sufficient to bring about the desired changes. My not seeing the kids while I'm claiming to be helping them, however, is sometimes very hard for their parents to accept.

There are times when therapists or counselors will recommend that your child take part in group psychotherapy, either as the single treatment of choice or in conjunction with some other type of treatment. This can be a very powerful form of therapy for kids who have a variety of problems. In group treatment, one or more therapists meet with several children at a time. There is generally at least one group session each week, although many groups meet more frequently.

The kids in these groups are roughly at the same age or developmental level, and are usually having similar difficulties. Much of the interaction takes place directly among the children themselves, rather than between the children and their therapists. For kids to be told by their peers that they are mishandling a situation is quite different than being told it by adult, authority figures. Even bitter medicine is usually much easier for them to swallow when it is delivered in this way. As trust develops within the group, a tremendous amount of support becomes available to all members in dealing with their individual problems. It becomes possible for each participant to benefit from the successes and failures of the other people in the group. The simple act of being with peers who have had similar experiences and who can discuss them from an insider's perspective is often highly beneficial.

MEDICATION

It is possible that your consultant could recommend that some type of medication might be helpful for your child. This suggestion can come up whether or not you have initially chosen to work with a child psychiatrist or a pediatric neurologist (medical doctors who, therefore, can write prescriptions for drugs). Although psychologists, social workers, guidance counselors, and most nurses are unable to prescribe medicines, they may recommend that you have your child evaluated by someone who can. Advice of this type is sometimes given when child specialists are dealing with such problems as depression and anxiety (for which pediatric psychiatrists are generally the best prescribers), or ADHD and Tourette's disorder (for which both pediatric psychiatrists and pediatric neurologists are appropriate).

     Many parents are initially put off when this subject is mentioned. Few of us would ever want to consider using a medication for our children if there were any way to avoid it. Rather than just ignoring the recommendation, however, it is important for you to find out all that you can about why it is being made. I've worked with children who have benefited tremendously from the judicious use of medication. Despite my conservative approach to this whole area, many children have told me that *they* truly value the changes that have been brought about through drug therapy. I would not be doing my job correctly if, on principle, I ignored a potential resource that can be helpful to children. This topic, perhaps more than any other involving a possible approach to your children's behavioral difficulties, requires that you take the time to educate yourself thoroughly before making any decisions.

Since we are troubleshooting, I will assume that you have told your counselor all about both the behavioral program and your child's continuing difficulties. If the counselor then suggests that the problem is severe enough to merit a medication evaluation for your child, it may help you to think of it as an evaluation for a medication *trial*. It is quite possible that the practitioner who is doing the evaluation will decide that drug therapy would not be helpful in improving your child's behavior. When there is actually a suggestion that a medication might be beneficial, it should generally be taken only as a recommendation that your child *try* it. You are absolutely free to disagree with, or choose to ignore, such advice. Discuss your reservations with the prescribing practitioner.

If you decide that a medication trial might be worthwhile, the same old rule about dropping things that aren't working applies here as much as anywhere else. In the event that the medicine isn't helping after sufficient time has gone by for it to do its work, you should inform the clinician who prescribed it and discuss any changes that need to be made. (This step is critically important. *Never* make changes in your child's medication on your own.) No practitioner would want a child to continue taking medication that isn't effective. It will also be helpful for you to keep in mind that most of these medicines are usually prescribed for limited periods, not for an entire lifetime.

Be prepared to ask plenty of questions when a helping professional suggests a medication trial for your child. Here are a few of my personal favorites: Why do you think that medication might be beneficial in this situation? Exactly what is it supposed to do? What are the expected and possible side effects? Are there any other alternatives? What is the recommended dosage and when should it be taken? Does it have to be taken during the school day and, if so, will the school nurse be able to administer it? How long will my child be taking this medicine? Is there any danger of possible abuse, addiction, or overdose? Can it be taken safely with other prescription or over-the-counter medications? You should ask the prescribing clinician every question that you can think of about the recommended medication and how it might affect your child.

There are also a number of other sources of information about psychopharmacology (the study of drugs that influence behavior and emotions) and psychoactive medications (the drugs themselves). In addition to the person who wrote the prescription, pharmacists will also be able to answer some of the questions that you might have. They will often provide you with the information sheets that are packaged with the medicines they sell (and which are reproduced in the *Physicians' Desk Reference,* described below).

Many books that include information about psychoactive medications are readily available through bookstores and libraries. Complete references for those on which I usually rely are included in the Bibliography. The one that I generally reach for first is the *Physicians' Desk Reference* (usually referred to as the "PDR"). This volume, which is updated each year, contains a huge amount of information that is provided by the pharmaceutical companies about each of their prescription drugs. Much of it is highly technical, and the complete lists of possible side effects for *any* of these medications can be scary. Remember that these lists usually contain every side effect that has ever been reported by anyone. The questions that come up when you are reading this type of book should be asked directly to your prescribing practitioner.

When I am in the mood to completely overdose on drug information, I refer to *The Practitioner's Guide to Psychoactive Drugs* and the *Practitioner's Guide to Psychoactive Drugs for Children and Adolescents*. These books provide a wealth of material about medications, the reasons for prescribing them in different situations, and the results that might be expected. Although they are written for professionals, much of the information can be useful to consumers as well.

USING OTHER RESOURCES IN THE COMMUNITY

If the troubleshooting process has gone well, you have now been able to improve your difficult child's behavior with the help of a counselor or therapist. Unfortunately, this will not always be the case. As a practicing psychologist, I hate to admit that your chosen professional might not have been able to get the child-behavioral-job done. I have to be honest, though. Although it grieves me to say so, sometimes this is the case for even the most skillful and well-intentioned of practitioners. Why, I might have found myself in this very situation from time to time. Not that I'll admit to it in public, of course.

The fact of the matter is that there are times when the sessions in a therapist's office will not be enough to help improve a difficult child's behavior. It has been my experience that this occurs more frequently in work with older children. Even this unfortunate turn of events, however, doesn't mean that there is nothing further that you can do. Sometimes, even the helpers need to call for help. You may already have had some experience with this if it was suggested that you visit another practitioner for a medication evaluation.

When the problems have not improved following your troubleshooting and consulting a child and family specialist, it is time to look for other sources of help. I know how frustrating it can be to have done a great deal of work in support of your children and to have gotten less than the desired results. Although it is the parents who are most directly affected, this situation can be awfully frustrating to their psychologists as well. It may sound too easy for me to say this from the distant security of my office chair, but please don't give up. There are still a number of steps that you can take, and it is always possible that the very next one might make the difference between failure and success.

The remaining approaches to helping your difficult child behave all make use of resources that are available in most communities, but not in the offices of individual therapists. Although you will eventually contact the providers of these services directly, it is always my recommendation that you first discuss such plans with your counselor. It is possible that there are other, more appropriate alternatives available to you. There can also be unforeseen consequences when you seek assistance from some outside agencies. This is not to say that these referrals should be avoided, but only that you should approach them as an educated consumer.

Most child and family practitioners have had experience in dealing with the other service providers in their communities. They will be able to tell you what assistance you can expect, and what problems you should be prepared for, when you become involved with these agencies. For example, it may be important for you to consult an attorney before making certain treatment decisions regarding your children. A good child and family specialist will either have this type of information on hand, or will know how to obtain it quickly.

DAY TREATMENT PROGRAMS

The next level of assistance that might be available in your community is provided by services generally called "day treatment programs," "day hospitals," or "partial hospitalization programs." As always, the possibility of using such agencies should first be thoroughly discussed with your counselor or therapist. In this type of approach, your child spends a part of each weekday participating in an intense, psychotherapeutic program. Treatment is not limited to the single hour that is usually provided by individual therapists, and there are a number of counselors and children involved at the same time. Since the kids come home when the program ends every day, these services should not be confused with residential programs.

Day treatment facilities are always staffed with several child specialists, generally from a variety of professional backgrounds. Although individual psychotherapy is ordinarily a part of these programs, groups of children also take part in some therapeutic services and activities. For instance, since the kids in a given day program are roughly the same age and have common concerns, it is usual for them to take part in daily group therapy sessions. It would be very difficult for most individual practitioners to provide this type of group treatment at such a frequency.

Day hospitals are total therapeutic environments, and children are completely immersed in treatment whenever they attend. Although there are usually a number of different activities going on each day, they are all intended to support the goal of bringing about behavioral and emotional change. Many of these programs take place each afternoon, when the school day is over. Some are scheduled only in the evenings. Others, which children attend for the whole day, actually include a fully accredited school. Day treatment is generally available throughout the year. You should expect that other family members will also be involved with the day hospital program to some degree. This participation often takes the form of groups for parents, siblings, or entire families. Again, I recommend that you discuss the details of each available partial hospitalization program with your therapist or counselor in order to select the one that best suits the particular needs of your family.

THE COURTS

Most of us, unless we are lawyers, generally try to avoid the court system as if it were the plague. This is especially true when it comes to situations involving our children. The *last* thing that we want is to get that dreaded phone call that begins, "Hi. I'm at the police station." Involvement with the judicial system often means other people will be making decisions that directly affect our families. This can be very uncomfortable, since our influence on the decision-making process may be extremely limited. If we are placed in this position involuntarily, as the result of a crime or a civil matter, we must rely on our lawyers and hope for the best.

Unfortunately, we are so conditioned to think of the courts only in terms of judging innocence or guilt that we rarely notice the other services that they can provide. When our involvement with the legal system is voluntary, the situation is quite a bit different. This is a very important fact to remember when you are trying to help your difficult child behave and nothing at all is working.

In most areas, it is either the family court or the juvenile court that provides assistance with children's behavioral problems. You should not even consider approaching these agencies for help until you have exhausted all of the other resources which have previously been discussed here. There are two reasons for this caution. First, the court system is tremendously overburdened. It already gets to deal with more than enough children, and doesn't need to drum up any extra business. This is not to say that you shouldn't make use of this resource if it becomes necessary. After all, you are paying for court services through your tax dollars. The judicial system should only become an option, however, when all of your previous troubleshooting efforts have failed.

The second reason to be cautious is that, despite your approaching the court as a voluntary consumer of its services, you will still be inviting outside authorities to become involved with your family. In this case, that authority will ultimately have the power of the law behind it. Although you may never interact directly with a judge, there is always one somewhere behind the scenes. Keep in mind that this can be a very positive circumstance when you are dealing with extremely difficult, or even dangerous, child behavior. Use of this resource requires a deliberate and educated approach on your part, however. The first step is to talk with your therapist or counselor about any plans for contacting the court. Make sure that you fully discuss all of the potential benefits and pitfalls of becoming involved with the judicial system. I *always* recommend that before signing anything that grants the court a role in helping you with your children, you consult an attorney.

The type of aid that family or juvenile courts can provide goes by different names in different states, and the exact procedures can vary as well. It is generally called a "Person in Need of Supervision Petition," a "Family with Service Needs Petition," or something similar. If you telephone the court and ask about this type of petition, they will be able to direct your call appropriately. When you file such a petition, you are basically saying to the court that you are have a family situation in which there is a minor child who is out of control. It is a request for the court to use legal means as a way of reestablishing your authority in the household and of helping your child to behave. Filings of this sort can be done by the child's legal custodian or guardian, whether married or single.

Once the petition has been filed, the case is usually assigned to a juvenile probation officer. This person interviews all of the involved family members and investigates other sources of relevant information. For example, school records are often reviewed. There may be contact with the family's therapists or with any other branches of the legal system that might be concerned. The probation officer then works with the family to develop a plan for getting the child's behavior back under control. This frequently takes the form of a contract with the child, which clearly specifies the behavior that will be expected.

What sets this approach apart from the usual behavioral program is that the expectations are not only those of the parents, but those of the court as well. The probation officer checks at regular intervals to make sure that the terms of the contract are being upheld. If the child's behavior improves, there is generally no further legal action and the case is closed. Violation of such a contract, however, can result in penalties much more severe than those discussed in Chapter 4. Failure to abide by these rules may lead the child directly to an appearance before a judge. The title "judge" is not an accidental one. When they are called upon, these court officials make decisions that _will_ be carried out. At the furthest extreme, a judge can even order residential placement for a completely uncontrollable child.

So much for the "worst-case-scenario." I didn't mean to scare you! My description of this most severe situation is not meant to discourage you from using a court's services. It's just to let you know that, while the judicial system can be a valuable tool, it is a tool whose power must be respected. Although such placement is one possible outcome, it is neither frequent nor desirable. The development of a legally binding behavioral contract is ordinarily enough to bring about the desired results.

Family and juvenile courts generally work closely with parents (and therapists) in constructing the contract. Such a process will allow you to make good use of the expertise that you have gained through designing your own behavioral program. For instance, the individual contract items can be exactly the same as your Target Goals. You might also be able to use the Reward and Penalty system that has become so familiar to your family. It is even possible that the probation officer could encourage you to run the program exactly as you designed it. The only difference might be that continuing, major behavioral problems will lead your child to become increasingly involved with the court system.

I often feel compelled to counteract some parents' image of a court eager to take away their children by any available means. It's important to keep in mind that the judicial system is already responsible for a lot of children that it would rather be without. Court officials must struggle to deal with large numbers of complicated cases involving those kids who have been genuinely neglected or abused. The state has no interest in assuming the guardianship of any more children than is absolutely necessary. Further, you should know that there are times when I directly suggest to parents that they file a petition requesting services from the court. These cases involve children who will not respond to any approach that doesn't have some real, external "teeth" in it. I've worked closely with a number of excellent probation officers who have used the court's power to support a family's behavioral work. They are sometimes in a position to help bring about improvements that might not otherwise have been possible.

EMERGENCY ROOMS AND PSYCHIATRIC HOSPITALS

If your child loses behavioral control to such an extent that there is imminent danger of harm to that child or to someone else, do not pass "Go," do not collect $200, but immediately contact your nearest hospital emergency room. If you can call a psychiatric hospital that has emergency services, so much the better. If there is a nearby psychiatric hospital that has emergency services *and* expertise in working with children and adolescents, that is the place to call. The important thing is to get help as quickly as possible from those professionals who are trained to deal with behavioral and emotional crises.

When children arrive at a hospital in this type of crisis, the first order of business for the staff is generally to get their behavior back under control. This can be done through verbal interaction, medication, or a combination of approaches. What happens next depends upon the overall circumstances. The family might be sent home with no further services to be provided by the hospital. Follow-up visits to the emergency room, or to a hospital mental health clinic, could be recommended. A referral to a therapist or counselor in the community is often made. If the situation is serious enough, the child could be admitted to the hospital for further treatment. Emergency rooms and general hospitals sometimes refer children to specialized, psychiatric hospitals when longer-term care is required.

In the event that a hospital admission is recommended, you should again adopt your consumer attitude after the initial crisis has passed. The questions that you should ask are similar to those which relate to private practitioners and medication. Why does the staff think that hospitalization might be beneficial at this point? Exactly what is it supposed to accomplish? Are there any other alternatives? Who will be working with my child? What is the staff's training and experience in working with children and families? What general approach do they take in dealing with children's behavioral and emotional problems? Is school work included in the hospital program? How long will my child be here? What kind of aftercare will be available? You should consult any therapists that have been working with your family and find out everything possible about the facility before making any decisions regarding hospitalization. It is important to keep in mind that if you and the hospital disagree strongly enough about how the case should be handled, legal action might be the result.

Psychiatric hospitalization can also be recommended for a child when there is not an acute, behavioral crisis in progress. This suggestion is generally made by a therapist or counselor who has been working with the family on an ongoing basis. When children become so gravely disabled by their emotional problems that they can no longer take care of themselves appropriately, inpatient treatment may become the approach of choice. This might also be the case if a child's continuing, uncontrolled behavior has resulted in a "chronic crisis." The longer-term hospital care that may be required in these situations is equivalent to residential treatment, which is discussed in the next section. Again, such an option always needs to be thoroughly explored and considered before it is chosen.

RESIDENTIAL TREATMENT PROGRAMS

The last topic in this chapter is always the least pleasant to contemplate. Residential placement. The phrase, itself, causes an immediate, negative reaction among almost all parents, no matter how difficult their child's behavior. In residential treatment, a child leaves home to live full-time at the facility where the program is located. What we will be discussing here is truly the last resort. It is the option that should be considered only when all of the other possibilities have been exhausted.

While most parents cringe at the idea of having a child removed from the household, there may come a time when placement in a residential treatment program is the only remaining alternative. You should know that these programs are generally not the nightmarish places that parents can imagine them to be. This has nothing at all to do with jail, juvenile detention, or reform school. The emphasis here is on *treatment,*

not punishment. A decision to consider residential placement should be thoroughly discussed with your therapist or
counselor. It is also important to obtain detailed information
about all of the available programs and to visit the ones that
appear to be the most appropriate.

The biggest advantage that residential facilities have
over parents, individual therapists, and day treatment programs is that they get to interact with the kids on a 24-hour
basis. Behavioral improvement is always the focus whenever
the children are awake. You should look for a placement that
includes a good academic program as well as a behavioral
treatment plan that will be developed specifically for your
child. Find out exactly what they think that they can do for
you and your family. Staff members should represent a variety
of clinical backgrounds, but they should all have specific expertise in working with difficult children. Ask about whether
other family members will be expected to participate in the
program. Policies regarding home visits should be explored,
including whether there will be an enforceable contract
specifying the child's expected behavior when at home. Are
there other children at the facility whose parents would be
willing to talk to you about their experiences with the program? Ask about everything! There is no reason to be shy
when you are facing such an important decision.

Over the years, I've been involved with a number of
families who have placed children in residential treatment
programs. They usually start out by experiencing the placement as a failure of their parenting. I seldom believe this to be
the case, since they have most likely tried every other possible approach before ever considering residential treatment.
To me, the behavioral program and the troubleshooting
process represent caring, involved parenting at its best. It just
might be that the problem is too big to handle at home. Residential placement should not be looked at as the end of the
world, but as another tool at your disposal. If your child's

behavior is severely negative, and if a residential program might help to improve such behavior, it is certainly in the child's best interests for you to consider treatment outside of your home.

The parents with whom I've worked have almost always assumed that, by turning to residential placement, they would be sending their child away forever. This is a most unlikely outcome. You may have noticed that, no matter where they've gone, your kids have usually been able to find their way home. You can expect this to be the case when they enter residential treatment as well. The goal of any ethical program is always to get the children home, with improved behavior, as soon as possible. A reputation for such good, rapid work will ensure that they continue to get referrals (from people like you and me) in the future. Ask the case managers how long they expect the treatment to take. Then make sure that you get regular feedback about your child's progress.

"Will my child hate me forever because of this?" This is the big question that's on the minds of almost all parents who place their child in a residential program. If your child doesn't already have extremely negative feelings toward you, it is unlikely that placement, by itself, will lead you to become permanent enemies. That's not to say that there won't be some real excitement around the decision to use residential treatment. The majority of children with whom I've worked, however, have made themselves comfortable at their placements, and have later acknowledged to me that their parents did the right thing. Of course, they might not have admitted this directly to their parents. No use in giving away good ammunition!

Here's a comparison that might be helpful. If your child has a physical illness that can only be cured by foul-tasting medicine, you have two choices. You can go along with the child's loud refusals to take the medicine, and let the sickness continue. Wrong! To help the child, you must take the chance that some anger will be aimed in your direction when you insist that the medicine be swallowed. *That's* good parenting. It is an easy matter to substitute "behavioral problem" for "physical illness," and "residential placement" for "foul-tasting medicine," in this little example.

Finally, I again want to emphasize that the choice of using a residential treatment program should never be made lightly. It should be considered only when all of your other troubleshooting efforts have failed, and when your child's negative behavior continues to be truly severe. How does this approach usually turn out? As with any form of therapy, there is never a guarantee of positive results. In the course of my work, however, I have known many children whose behavior improved significantly as a result of residential treatment.

Secret Stuff

If we were working together in my office, you wouldn't hear anything about this "secret stuff" until your program had been successfully running for a week or two. You should use your willpower, skip to the Epilogue now, and save this chapter until you have fine-tuned your own program. Of course, I have to be realistic about this. The chances of your not immediately reading a chapter called "Secret Stuff" are pretty slim.

On the surface, we have been involved in designing, constructing, and running a program to help your difficult child behave. This is actually only a part of what has been happening, and it may be the smallest part. In truth, your approach to parenting has also been influenced by a behavioral program. There are Rewards and Penalties for you just like those that you developed for your child. If you have become more consistent and unified in your approach to discipline, you have been rewarded by significant improvements in your child's behavior. If you have not stuck to the recommended program, or if you have become less consistent in its application over time, you will be penalized by the return or continuation of your child's negative behavior. I hope that such a Penalty will lead you to reexamine your program in order to correct any problems.

My experience has taught me that only a very small percentage of children's behavioral difficulties are due to something that is actually wrong with the child. It is most often the interactions between children and the important adults in their lives that lead to problems. While it is certainly true that many factors can be involved in the development of negative behavior, it is also true that consistent and unified parenting will be beneficial for children under any circumstances.

There is little chance that through your use of this or any other book you will be able to raise children who always behave perfectly. I don't know of _any_ children who always behave perfectly. On the other hand, it is quite likely that the approach described here has led to genuine improvements in your children's behavior. It is no secret at all that your good parenting has made the difference.

*F*arewell to Bryan

Whatever became of Bryan, our eight-year-old, hypothetical child? Cases involving hypothetical children always turn out very well. Not surprisingly, Bryan's treatment was 100 percent successful. He became a model son and student, graduating *magna cum laude* from Harvard. At this point, he is the president of either a major corporation or a very large country (I haven't yet decided which). Bryan greatly honored me by naming his first child after me. He had a little girl who is now, unfortunately, known only as "Schwarz." I would like to publicly express my appreciation to Bryan for his unstinting and selfless participation in this project.

AND TO YOU

You have done a tremendous amount of work in designing, constructing, and running your program. It is my fondest hope that the results of your labors will be similar to those that I have seen in my work with families. I am convinced that almost all children want to behave well. Some have waited years for their parents to become unified and consistent enough to provide them with clear guidelines for acceptable behavior. Children rejoice in their parents' praise and in their own sense of mastery and self-control. I wish you continued success in helping your children behave.

Resources for Special Needs

ATTENTION-DEFICIT HYPERACTIVITY DISORDER

Children and Adults with Attention Deficit Disorders (CH.A.D.D.):

CH.A.D.D. is a nonprofit, parent-based organization formed to better the lives of individuals with attention-deficit disorders and those who care for them. By means of family support and advocacy, public and professional education, and encouragement of scientific research, CH.A.D.D. works to ensure that those with attention deficit disorders reach their inherent potential. CH.A.D.D. is an international organization with over 600 local chapters and almost 30,000 members. Through informative monthly meetings with guest speakers, newsletters, and the caring of other parents, CH.A.D.D. members form a close network to exchange helpful ideas about raising a child with an attention deficit disorder. CH.A.D.D. can be reached at 499 N.W. 70th Avenue, Suite 109, Plantation, FL 33317, (305) 587-3700. They will send you general information and put you in touch with a local chapter.

Attention Deficit Disorder (ADD) Forum on the CompuServe Information Service:

If you have a computer and a modem, you can join this international, 24-hour-a-day, ADD support group with over 24,000 members from the U. S., Argentina, Ireland, U. K., Germany, Australia, Canada, Belgium, France, Netherlands, Luxembourg, South Africa, Scotland, and Norway. In their message area, you'll find messages from members on a wide variety of topics. They also have libraries that contain files, reports, discussions, and other useful information uploaded to the forum by its members. A conference area is divided into multiple rooms in which members are invited to discuss various issues, which vary from room to room. For information on joining CompuServe, call (800) 848-8199. To get to the ADD Forum, type GO ADD <Enter>.

alt.support.attn-deficit:

This is another resource for the computer and modem crowd. For those who have access to the Internet, this Usenet newsgroup provides an open forum for posting and reading messages about all aspects of attention deficit disorders.

TOURETTE'S DISORDER

Tourette Syndrome Association, Inc. (TSA):

TSA publishes an excellent newsletter, with a uniquely high standard of accuracy and informativeness, that reaches over 30,000 people in the United States and abroad. They have a large number of publications, films, programs, and services that address Tourette's disorder and the behaviors sometimes associated with it (for example, problems with learning, attention, obsessions, and impulse control). TSA can be reached at 42-40 Bell Boulevard, Bayside, NY 11361, (800) 237-0717 outside of New York State and (718) 224-2999 in New York. You will receive general information, the name of the contact person for your local affiliate, and a referral list of physicians.

alt.support.tourette:

If you have a computer, a modem, and access to the Internet, this Usenet newsgroup provides an open forum for posting and reading messages about all aspects of Tourette's disorder.

Bibliography

Here are the books that were useful to me in developing this approach to helping your difficult child behave. I certainly don't agree with everything that is in each of them (as if this would come as a surprise to you by now), but each one provides at least some interesting information to consider. Several of the authors have written many books, and there are many other books available about each subject, but the listed title is a good place to start. My comments follow each reference citation.

American Psychiatric Association. *Diagnostic and Statistical Manual of Mental Disorders.* 4th ed. Washington, DC: American Psychiatric Association, 1994.

>   Descriptions of, and information about, all currently classified psychiatric disorders. This book is intended for use in making diagnoses and does not include material regarding treatment.

Bandura, Albert. *Social Learning Theory.* Englewood Cliffs, NJ: Prentice-Hall, 1977.

>   Social learning theory, from the horse's mouth.

Berkow, Robert, ed. *The Merck Manual of Diagnosis and Therapy.* 16th ed. Rahway, NJ: Merck Research Laboratories, 1992.

>   Complete, technical discussions of what appear to be all of the illnesses known to humankind and how to cure them. It is written for medical personnel, but it contains much that is understandable to the rest of us. The book includes information about children's behavioral, emotional, and neurological problems. Warning: If you

are at all prone to picking up symptoms that you read about, stay away from this one!

Comings, David E. *Tourette Syndrome and Human Behavior.* Duarte, CA: Hope Press, 1990.

> This is a comprehensive book about Tourette's disorder, written from the perspective of a human geneticist.

Faber, Adele and Mazlish, Elaine. *Siblings Without Rivalry: How to Help Your Children Live Together So You Can Live Too.* New York: Avon, 1987.

> A wonderful book that I frequently recommend in my practice. If you have more than one child, you should definitely know about this one. It can really help.

Geisel, Theodor Seuss [Dr. Seuss]. *Horton Hatches the Egg.* New York: Random House, 1940.

> An early, and highly influential, study of good and bad single-parenting.

Gelenberg, Alan J.; Bassuk, Ellen L.; and Schoonover, Stephen C., eds. *The Practitioner's Guide to Psychoactive Drugs.* 3rd ed. New York: Plenum Medical Book Company, 1991.

> My Bible when it comes to this subject. Covers it all.

Medical Economics Data Production Company. *Physicians' Desk Reference.* 48th ed. Montvale, NJ: Medical Economics Data Production Company, 1994.

> Information from the pharmaceutical companies about each of their prescription medicines.

Patterson, Gerald R. *Living with Children: New Methods for Parents and Teachers,* Revised. Champaign, IL: Research Press, 1976.

> A behavioral program that is closely based on learning theory. It provides traditional definitions of the various tools for improving behavior. This was an early influence on the book that you are now holding.

Piaget, Jean. *Biology and Knowledge.* Chicago: University of Chicago Press, 1971.

> How children's thinking develops into that of adults.

Skinner, B. F. *Beyond Freedom and Dignity.* New York: Knopf, 1971.
Skinnerian behaviorism, from the horse's mouth.

Taylor, John F. *Helping Your Hyperactive/Attention Deficit Child.* Rocklin, CA: Prima Publishing, 1994.
This is a comprehensive guide to ADHD, with a large number of helpful suggestions.

Werry, John S. and Aman, Michael G., eds. *Practitioner's Guide to Psychoactive Drugs for Children and Adolescents.* New York: Plenum Medical Book Company, 1993.
My Bible when it comes to this part of the subject. Covers it all.

Index

About the Author

Michael Schwarzchild, Ph.D., is a clinical psychologist with a private practice in Brookfield, Connecticut. After receiving his B.A. in theatre from Bennington College, he attended Fordham University, where he received his M.A. and Ph.D. in psychology. As a psychologist, he has worked in psychiatric and general hospitals, a physical rehabilitation center, a private school (for children with learning disabilities, speech disorders, and/or behavioral problems), a child guidance center, and a mental health clinic. He has also taught undergraduate classes in psychology. Dr. Schwarzchild currently provides individual, couples, and family psychotherapy while working with children, adolescents, and adults.